W9-AZO-887

Gerry Faust's
Tales from the
Notre Dame
Sideline

Gerry Faust, John Heisler, and Bob Logan

www.SportsPublishingLLC.com

ISBN: 1-58261-399-0

All photos are courtesy of the University of Notre Dame Sports Information Department.

Publisher: Peter L. Bannon
Senior managing editor: Susan M. Moyer
Acquisitions editor: Mike Pearson
Developmental editor: Noah Amstadter
Art director: K. Jeffrey Higgerson
Dust jacket design: Kenneth J. O'Brien
Project manager: Alicia Wentworth
Imaging: Christine Mohrbacher, Kerri Baker
        Kenneth J. O'Brien, Dustin Hubbart
Photo editor: Erin Linden-Levy
Copy editor: Cynthia L. McNew
Vice president of sales and marketing: Kevin King
Media and promotions managers: Cory Whitt (regional),
        Randy Fouts (national), Maurey Williamson (print)

Printed in the United States of America

Sports Publishing L.L.C.
804 North Neil Street
Champaign, IL 61820

Phone: 1-877-424-2665
Fax: 217-363-2073
Web site: www.SportsPublishingLLC.com

To Father Hesburgh and Father Joyce, who gave me the opportunity to be part of Notre Dame for five years. To my mom and dad, who gave me my faith and my foundation and loved me always through their lives. To my wife Marlene, who for 41 years has been my biggest supporter. To my children and their spouses: Julie Marie and husband Steve, Gerry III and wife Dee Dee, and Steve and wife Pij. And to my grandchildren, Megan Marie, Natalie Marie, Alexandra Michelle, Chloe Frances and Spencer. Other than my faith, my family is the most important part of my life.

—G.F.

For two Notre Dame men—Ray Meyer and Joe Boland. Coach Ray, a tower of class and integrity for 42 years at DePaul, is a great man—words I do not use lightly. I am proud to hear him call me a friend. I never met Joe Boland, but hearing his stirring radio calls of Notre Dame games as a boy in Philadelphia gave me a lifetime appreciation of the Fighting Irish tradition and what this university stands for.

Also, it has been a pleasure working with Coach Gerry Faust and John Heisler, two of Notre Dame's finest people.

—B.L.

To my wife Karen, the best editor and proofreader a writer could ever ask for, and to everyone who has ever played or coached football for the Irish—without their passion for Notre Dame football, there would be no tales to tell.

—J.H.

Contents

Acknowledgments vii

Chapter 1
The Greatest Notre Dame Team of All Time 1

Chapter 2
The Era of Ara 3

Chapter 3
A Devine Time 19

Chapter 4
Faust Start, Frustrating Finish 36

Chapter 5
My Dream Didn't Last 56

Chapter 6
Holtz, That Tiger 74

Chapter 7
A Lou's Who of Irish Talent .95

Chapter 8
Play Like a Champion This Season 114

Chapter 9
Davie's Irish—Highs and Lows 129

Chapter 10
Ty's Not Playing for a Tie 149

Chapter 11
Willing Hands Help Willingham 162

Chapter 12
The Greatest Games 178

Chapter 13
The Irish Spirit 200

Acknowledgments

The greatness of Notre Dame comes from its people. Not only the professors and administrators, but all the people at the University, in every capacity that you can think of. They are the people who make Notre Dame great. Every time I call or go on the campus, or make a visit, people go out of their way to help people. They love their jobs, they love their atmosphere, and they love Notre Dame. These people work there because they want to be there, because they have a feeling for what Notre Dame stands for. No other university can match that type of mystique. I personally want to thank all the people at Notre Dame, from the groundskeeper to the president, to the chairman of the board, because their mission is to help people become better people in life. Every person has his or her niche. And without each person, the whole university would not be what it is today. Notre Dame receives its greatness from its people.

I want to specifically thank John Heisler for his contributions in making this book possible. John is the best sports information director in the country and possesses the unique ability to express in words what Notre Dame football is all about. Without his expertise, knowledge and hard work, this book would not have been written. Bob Logan, one of the best sportswriters in the country, did a tremendous job of putting the book together. The best way to describe Bob Logan is that he's a real pro in the sportswriting world. Last but not least, Noah Amstadter, Notre Dame Class of 2002, put his heart and soul into this book. Without Noah, this book would still be in the formulating process. Notre Dame football has made this book possible, for without its mystique, tradition and history there would be no reason to write this book.

—Gerry Faust

CHAPTER 1

The Greatest
Notre Dame Team
of All Time

Faust Fodder

Everyone, after reading the title of this chapter, probably started choosing his or her favorite group of Notre Dame players. Very recently, something happened that made me realize what, to me, is Notre Dame's greatest team.

On May 5, 2004, as I was flying on Mike Leep's airplane to South Bend, we were 13,000 feet above and 25 miles away from our destination. As I sat behind our pilots, Mark Jamieson and John MacDonald, I looked out the front of the plane and saw the sun shining off the Golden Dome.

I reflected back to the five years I spent at Notre Dame under the greatest team, university president Father Ted Hesburgh and executive vice president Father Ned Joyce. For 35 years a total team, they brought Notre Dame to a higher level of greatness through their leadership.

Tears came to my eyes, for the reason I was going to South Bend was to attend the funeral mass of Father Joyce.

When I arrived, Mike Leep and I went to the Grotto behind the Basilica of the Sacred Heart. When walking to the Basilica, after keeping my promise to Our Lady of always going to the Grotto first when I was at Notre Dame, Mike said to me, "There's Father Hesburgh."

I yelled, "Father Hesburgh!" And I ran up to him as he was going to the Basilica for the funeral mass of Father Joyce.

He came up to me and said, "Gerry, I knew you would be here."

Tears came to my eyes because I knew the greatest team was now separated from one another. One in heaven, the other still on Earth carrying out Christ's work. Yes, the greatest Notre Dame team was Hesburgh and Joyce.

✝

CHAPTER 2

The Era of Ara

Faust Fodder

In 1955 Coach Ara Parseghian was the head football coach at Miami University in Oxford, Ohio, and I
was a quarterback at the University of Dayton. He and
some of his coaches came up to scout us in our spring
game because Dayton played Miami every fall. I did not
participate in the spring game that year because I had
hurt my knee in practice and I was on crutches.

I was standing near the bench when along came
Coach Parseghian. He came up to me and asked me
how my knee was. I said, "Fine." He wished me good
luck and he asked me my name.

I told him I was Gerry Faust, and he knew that I
played quarterback.

Soon after, Ara left Miami to become the head
coach at Northwestern, where he stayed until coming
to Notre Dame in 1964. After I graduated, I served as
an assistant coach at my alma mater, Chaminade High
School in Dayton, for two years before becoming the

head coach at Moeller in Cincinnati in 1960. I stayed there until I took the Notre Dame job in 1980, and during that time Coach Parseghian recruited several of our players at Moeller.

Who would ever have thought on that spring day in 1955 when we two were talking that Ara Parseghian and Gerry Faust would each someday be the head football coach at the University of Notre Dame? Coach Parseghian and I both were born on May 21. We have the same birthday and we're both from Ohio—and we each became the head coach at Notre Dame.

✜

At the Beginning

Ara Parseghian's success as head coach at Northwestern—including four consecutive victories over Notre Dame (1960-63)—prompted him to consider other options in the college game as the 1963 season came to a close. Knowing the Irish had an interim coach, Hugh Devore, in 1963, Parseghian placed a phone call to Notre Dame executive vice president Rev. Edmund P. Joyce, C.S.C., to inquire about the University's future plans for the job. While Parseghian was interested, Father Joyce was noncommittal.

Meanwhile, Parseghian also pursued the vacancy at Miami of Florida and was headed to Coral Gables to interview for that opening when he called home while in St. Louis between flights. Told by wife Katie that Father Joyce had called, Parseghian promptly took the next flight back to South Bend. He first met Father Joyce in Chicago in early December following the Notre Dame Club of Chicago's annual Rockne Awards Dinner, then later visited with him in New York in conjunction with the annual National Football Foundation dinner. Another Chicago meeting with Father Joyce and president Rev. Theodore M. Hesburgh, C.S.C., came next, eventually Ara was hired—and the rest is history.

Finding Tradition

Ara Parseghian was no stranger to Notre Dame football when he became the Irish head coach prior to the 1964 season. But even after earning the attention of Irish fans when his Northwestern teams knocked off Notre Dame four straight times, the early fervor of the Irish students impressed him:

"The first time I ever came to campus after I was hired, they introduced me at halftime of a basketball game. The kids stood up and gave me a 15-minute ovation. I was surprised but thought it was just a flurry of enthusiasm. A few weeks later one of the dorms held an impromptu pep rally outside in 28-degree weather. There must have been hundreds of kids there all yelling like mad. I'd never seen anything like it. I'd heard about Notre Dame tradition, but I didn't know it could be like that."

Bob Gladieux: Little Guy, Big Contributions

Bob Gladieux made arguably the biggest play in the biggest game in one of the biggest seasons in the history of Notre Dame football.

And to think that the Louisville, Ohio, product wasn't originally convinced he was big enough to make a dent in the Irish lineup.

Eventually listed at 5'11" and 185 pounds, he originally showed up in the line to play halfback in 1965 for Notre Dame head coach Ara Parseghian while weighing about 165.

"Right away I decided I was in the wrong place. The kid in front of me weighed 218 pounds. If these are the halfbacks, I thought to myself, what am I doing here?" Gladieux recalls.

But he quickly proved he belonged:

"I think it might be said that Bob was saved by his own ignorance. I mean ignorance in the sense of not being aware of the obstacles that confronted him," says Gladiuex's classmate and offensive tackle George Kunz.

"We freshmen were in a Monday scrimmage against the varsity guys who had not played the previous Saturday, and they let us return a kickoff. I had tried to throw a block and was lying on the ground when Gladieux came through there. Bob was running hard, veering to his right on this varsity guy who had the angle. Then—zoom—he did all right, even if he did weigh only 165."

Gladieux, who acquired the nickname Harpo based on his hair and Harpo Marx-like looks, earned his stripes in practices against a bunch of All-Americans on the other side of the line.

"I realized I wasn't too small in my freshman year. I was on the prep team—we simulated the next opponent's offense—and I played against Kevin Hardy, Alan Page, Pete Duranko and the rest of that group. That's a good way for a little guy to break in," he said.

A little more than a year later, Gladieux scored Notre Dame's only touchdown in the monumental 10-10 tie with unbeaten Michigan State in East Lansing—in a game that pre-served Irish national titles hopes that came true after a 51-0 win a week later at USC.

Gladieux's chance came when Irish All-America halfback Nick Eddy slipped stepping off the train in East Lansing the day before the game and re-injured an already banged-up shoulder and leg.

"About five minutes before the game, coach told me I was starting," says Gladiuex.

His name didn't dominate the final stat sheet—he rushed one time for one yard, but led Irish receivers with three grabs for 71 yards. After the Spartans had taken a 10-0 second-period lead, he and quarterback Coley O'Brien—another injury fill-in after Terry Hanratty's first-period shoulder injury—quickly responded.

After a first-down incompletion, O'Brien threw to Gladieux for 11 yards. After another completion for nine yards to Rocky Bleier at the Michigan State 34, on second and one O'Brien zeroed in on Gladieux at the goal line. Gladieux's toughest challenge from there was to negotiate his way around the goal-post standard. Joe Azzaro's extra point cut the Spartan lead to 10-7 and Azzaro's field goal on the first play on the final period provided the only other scoring the rest of the way.

So much for the little guy, who eventually came back to run a travel bureau in South Bend.

Irish vs. Keyes:
Mission Not Accomplished

Notre Dame's student newspaper, *The Observer*, decided to take matters into its own hands when the Irish played host to Purdue on the last Saturday in September of 1968. The Irish came into the contest ranked first in one wire-service poll, with the Boilermakers first in the other.

After Boiler star Leroy Keyes had helped beat Notre Dame in 1967 (a 28-21 Purdue win helped by a Keyes touchdown reception)—and tried it in '66 (in a 26-14 Irish victory he scored the first Boiler points on a 94-yard return of an errant pitch)—Notre Dame student journalists took no chances. In their Saturday gameday edition, they ran a 10-by-10-inch close-up mug shot of Keyes under the headline "GET THIS MAN." They detailed his aliases, the charge against him ("Assault with a deadly weapon known as The Pigskin"), his record ("Committed murder on the Irish Sept. 30, 1967; attempted murder on the Irish Sept. 24, 1966") and other "remarks" ("This criminal is armed and dangerous. Now in his third year of wanton destruction ...").

Keyes figured to contribute a little of everything after his '67 performance against Notre Dame in which he kicked off, returned punts and kickoffs, caught nine passes, threw a pass, rushed eight times, intercepted a pass and knocked down three others.

Alas, the ploy didn't work. Purdue defeated the Irish 37-22 and Keyes led the Boilers with 90 rushing yards, scored on runs of 16 and 18 yards and threw a 17-yard TD pass.

John Huarte: One Super Season

Let's be honest: there was no one on Notre Dame's list of 1964 football opponents living in fear over the prospect of facing senior quarterback John Huarte and the Fighting Irish.

After all, the Irish were coming off a 2-7 season in '63 under an interim coach. Notre Dame had been a combined 19-30 over the previous five seasons, none of them winning campaigns. How much could anyone expect from first-year Notre Dame coach Ara Parseghian or this little-used (he'd attempted 50 throws his first two seasons combined), seldom-heard-from veteran quarterback he tabbed to be his starter?

Irish fans—and college fans around the country—quickly found out. In the season opener, Notre Dame whipped Wisconsin 31-7, and in the process Huarte completed nine throws to split end Jack Snow for 217 yards (out of 270 total passing yards for the Irish). As the Irish sped to nine straight wins to open the seasons, Huarte sped to the Heisman Trophy, a destiny that might have seemed way off the map before that season began.

How did he do it? For one, he taped inside his locker a picture of a fox wearing glasses. Though his teammates razzed him about it, Huarte's response was: "Every day I'd look at the photo and remind myself that to succeed in this world you've just got to be as mentally sharp as that fox."

And Huarte spent much of his senior season explaining how his lack of playing time as a sophomore and junior did nothing to discourage him:

"That's ridiculous. You know you can do it. You can't quit on yourself because you have to be ready if a chance comes. In a running offense I wouldn't be as a good a quarterback because I'm a thrower, but our offense is ideal for me. For two years nothing happens, and then it blooms in one year. It's magic."

He didn't hesitate to identify the turning point in his Notre Dame career:

"Last December 14th or 15th [of 1963] I think it was. Most of the students had left for the holidays, but I still was on campus. And when I heard the announcement that Mr. Parseghian was the new football coach, I was confident that I would play a lot of football for Notre Dame."

And so he did—and well enough to outpoint a Heisman field that included names like Roger Staubach (he won it the year before in '63), Gale Sayers, Dick Butkus, Joe Namath, Craig Morton and Jerry Rhome (who finished second).

Huarte's season in the sun might have been even more unlikely than many ever knew considering the shoulder separation he suffered in spring practice. He had to talk doctors out of surgery in order to stay on the active roster.

For his part, Parseghian said the main thing he and his staff did was restore Huarte's confidence. Halfway through the '64 season, the Irish stood 5-0 after Huarte threw for 300 yards with 21 completions in a 28-6 win over Stanford. It didn't hurt that a week later, in a head-to-head matchup with Staubach and

Navy, the Irish prevailed 40-0 while Huarte completed 10 pass-es for 274 yards (still a Notre Dame record for average per completion).

At the time Huarte was announced as the Heisman winner, Notre Dame was still undefeated. Years later, the trophy sat atop the family piano, holding sheet music for daughter Bridget. John Huarte—Heisman Memorial Trophy winner.

It has a nice ring to it.

Two DiNardos and a Pomarico: They Made St. Francis Prep Proud

It's no simple trip from Brooklyn, New York, to South Bend, Indiana, but Ara Parseghian to this day remains particularly happy that a trio of standout offensive linemen from St. Francis Prep in Brooklyn decided to make Notre Dame their college football home.

First came offensive left guard Larry DiNardo, who led the Irish in playing time as a junior in '69, served as a team captain the following year and helped that '70 team establish a Notre Dame record with 510.5 yards of offense per game. A two-time All-American, he also earned Academic All-America honors on his way to a career in law.

Younger brother Gerry also played guard (but on the right side), from 1972 to '74, and he, too, helped the Irish set records. On their way to the national title in '73, the Irish set a single-season mark at Notre Dame with 3,502 ground yards. A consensus All-American, Gerry went into coaching and has served as head coach at Vanderbilt, LSU and currently Indiana.

After Larry graduated following the '70 season, fellow St. Francis alum Frank Pomarico took over the starting spot there for the next three seasons, captaining the Irish in 1973. Pomarico has remained in business in South Bend—and was

Ara Parseghian greets his 1970 captains, Larry DiNardo (left) and Tim Kelly.

named athletic director at St. Joseph's High School in South Bend in 2004.

"Larry wasn't the first from St. Francis to play football at Notre Dame, but when Larry graduated and won all the student-athlete awards, he made an impression on the school," said younger brother Gerry.

"When Frank and I were still in high school, we would always look forward to Larry coming back to talk to us and tell us about Notre Dame. Then Frank and I went back and did the same thing. These kids could see they could come to a place like Notre Dame. It wasn't just a dream for a boy from a small school in Brooklyn. It could be a reality."

Pomarico remembers Gerry as being something of an unlikely football star who played a year at a prep school because he never played much football until his senior year in high school:

"I remember Gerry was only five-three and 120 pounds when we entered high school. He made himself into a football player. It didn't come naturally for him."

Gerry credited Parseghian with his bent for coaching:

"After my college career was finished, I sat down and wrote Coach Parseghian a long letter and told him how much he meant to me. He's probably the main reason I'm in coaching."

Gerry got a taste of his brother's coaching style as a freshman when Larry helped out Parseghian's staff as a graduate assistant. Then Gerry got his feet wet as an assistant at Eastern Michigan under head coach Mike Stock, a former Irish assistant under Parseghian.

Larry remembers his high school days when football practices were anything but routine:

"My school didn't have a practice field so we actually went to practice on the elevated [train]. We went out to a distant station of Brooklyn, about a 45-minute train ride, carrying all the equipment. After practice each of us would go home from there."

Ara was glad they made it safely.

Rocky Bleier: He Came Back for More

He played on Notre Dame's 1966 national title team.
He served as captain of the 1967 Irish squad.

Not a bad college résumé for the guy who was listed as Robert or Bob in his college days as often as he was known as Rocky (his father, Bob Sr., gave him that name because he did- n't want him to be called Junior).

But it was the spirit in South Bend that convinced him to migrate from Appleton, Wisconsin, to the Notre Dame campus.

"This spirit is real. You've never seen anything like it. You really get a feeling when there are five or six thousand kids in that fieldhouse just yelling and cheering and the band is playing the Victory March. I know one guy who transferred to the University of Wisconsin, but he comes back here for football weekends, and he wouldn't miss a pep rally."

A stint in Vietnam and a stirring comeback from combat injuries to play and star for the Pittsburgh Steelers made him something of a legend in football circles.

Though he was one of Ara Parseghian's first recruits and played on Parseghian's first four Irish teams, demand for a 5'9", 183-pound running back wasn't huge.

Drafted by the military with two games to go in the '68 season, he entered the army with the idea of "serving my time and not getting hurt."

It didn't exactly happen that way. Serving in a reconnais- sance platoon in an area infiltrated by the North Vietnamese army, Bleier was shot in the left thigh, then suffered injuries to his right foot when it was hit by a grenade. The foot had been blown open—and bone spurs and scar tissue required two oper- ations to provide any mobility.

Cut from the Steelers on the final day in 1970 (he was a 16th-round draft pick), he went through another operation and finally came back to play, mostly on special teams, in 1971. He worked his way back into the mix well enough to finally earn a starting assignment in 1974, midway through his sixth season in the pros. Pittsburgh won Super Bowl titles with Bleier's help after the '75, '76, '79 and '80 seasons, and Bleier finished with 3,864 career rushing yards in the pros.

He wasn't sure he'd make it back from Vietnam in one piece. An American doctor, picking shrapnel out of his feet with a pair of forceps, said, "Rocky Bleier? Notre Dame captain?" When Bleier responded affirmatively, the doctor said, "I'm from USC. I was at the game you beat us 51-0." Bleier closed his eyes and said, "Oh, no."

A doctor from Thailand who had initially treated Bleier met him by chance at a banquet years later. "I felt he'd never carry the ball again," said Dr. Anan Laorr. "The way he's come back is remarkable."

Parseghian remembers Bleier returning to Notre Dame in 1969 to be introduced at halftime of an Irish home game not long after returning from Vietnam.

"I saw him limping down the hallway. As a young man and a player, he had all the right qualities. Yes, he was one of my favorite players. And I thought it was admirable that he was going to give football a try again. But I wondered to myself, 'Good Lord, how is he ever going to do it?'"

Bleier went on to a career as a television sportscaster and a motivational speaker.

"My biggest message is that the only constant in life is change and you have to be able to adapt to that change and believe in yourself. I tell people you can be the very best you can be; your destiny lies in your own hands," said Bleier.

"You have choices but you have to be willing to pay the price for that change, for what you want to do. A lot of people want to change but a lot of people aren't willing to pay that price and they don't have the confidence in themselves.

"I tell them that there's no magic out there, there are no lights you turn on or buttons you press or drugs you take."

Terry Hanratty:
Half of the "Fling/Cling" Duo

Notre Dame quarterback Terry Hanratty earned his share of nicknames in four years on the Irish campus.

They called him "The Rat"—close friend Ron Dushney tagged him with that one. They called him "Mr. Fling," the front end of the pass-catch tandem, with "Mr. Cling," receiver Jim Seymour. Some preferred "Butler Bullet" based on his western Pennsylvania roots.

At the end of it all, midway through his senior season in 1968, they called him Notre Dame's all-time leader in total offense—after he surpassed the total yardage figure of another former Irish star with a noteworthy nickname, George Gipp, also known as "The Gipper."

Good enough to make the cover of *Time* with Seymour as sophomore sensations in 1966, Hanratty mostly enjoyed a storybook career with the Irish. By the time he graduated he'd completed more passes than any other player to suit up for Notre Dame—and finished, in order, sixth, ninth and third in three Heisman Trophy votes in his three seasons as the regular at quarterback. It didn't hurt that the Irish won the national title along the way in his sophomore season.

Thirty-five years later, he stills holds the Irish single-game pass attempt mark (63 vs. Purdue in '67, helping him tie the NCAA single-game record for total offense attempts at 75), as well as season marks from '68 for both pass completions and attempts per game.

"He's the finest quarterback I've ever been associated with," said Irish offensive coordinator Tom Pagna at the time Gipp's total offense mark fell.

"For speed of the ball, distance, trajectory and relative accuracy, he's got the finest arm I've ever seen in college football."

High praise, indeed.

For Hanratty, the choice of colleges came down mainly to Notre Dame and Michigan State. If there was a difference at the end it was Ara Parseghian.

"Ara impressed me more than any person I've ever met in my life," Hanratty said in '76 when he and his Pittsburgh Steeler teammates were preparing to face a Parseghian-coached team in the College All-Star game in Chicago.

"Some other schools offered me a lot of things: wall-to-wall carpeting, furniture, a car. I don't know how at that age I turned it down, especially since I grew up without a dime.

"But Ara made it a privilege to go to Notre Dame. I talked to him, and that's where it was. At that time, I thought it was between Michigan State and Notre Dame. Then we met at lunch and it was all over. Dynamic person."

Hanratty laughs now remembering how Ara kept him humble:

"You have a tendency at that age to let your head get blown out of proportion. Ara is the type of man who wouldn't let that happen."

As Hanratty reiterated on camera in the epic video "Wake Up the Echoes," he would think he'd played well in a game until watching the film, at which time Ara would pick out the smallest of mistakes.

Hanratty says he most respected his head coach for insisting on knee surgery late in his senior year in '68.

"I told him, 'I can play against Southern Cal. The knee is getting stronger.' Ara told me, 'I'm not going to jeopardize it for one ballgame.'"

The Irish came into the '66 season with a rash of sophomores in key positions, but two of them—Hanratty and Seymour—wasted no time playing like grizzled veterans. In the season opener, against a Bob Griese-led Purdue team, Hanratty completed 16 of his 24 throws for 304 yards, with 13 of them ending up in the hands of Seymour for 276 yards and three scores. "They produced beyond my fondest hopes," said Parseghian after the 26-14 Irish win. "I was afraid I might be over-confident with these boys, but they showed everyone just how good they are."

That game marked the first that Hanratty's mother ever saw him play—she watched the game on television, refusing to ever come to any of his high school games for fear he would be hurt.

Amazingly, Hanratty wasn't sure he'd ever see the field in South Bend. As a freshman ineligible for varsity competition, he and classmate Coley O'Brien both figured they might play second fiddle to Tom Schoen, who was the backup signal caller as a sophomore in '67. But Schoen moved to safety for '68, Hanratty won the job—and the rest is history.

A Couple of Guys Named Joe

Ara Parseghian recruited plenty of guys named Joe during his 11 seasons at Notre Dame. But few loomed as large as Joe Theismann and Joe Montana, even though Montana's lone season with Ara came in Montana's '74 rookie year when freshmen were ineligible for varsity play.

Irish offensive coordinator Tom Pagna remembers standing on a hill in western Pennsylvania watching a summer camp session in which a high school quarterback was throwing to one of the clinic coaches, a guy named Rocky Bleier, a former Irish player then with the Pittsburgh Steelers. Standing with Pagna was another current Steeler, former Irish quarterback Terry Hanratty.

Said Hanratty, "Who is that guy?"

"I'm recruiting him," said Pagna. "His name is Joe Montana."

"Sounds like a gunfighter," said Hanratty.

Years earlier it was Theismann, then an inexperienced sophomore, who was filling in for an injured Hanratty in '68 as the Irish finished the season at USC. Theismann's first throw on the very first play of the game was intercepted by the Trojans and returned for a score.

Theismann's response? "Don't worry, Coach. That was just one pass in the game. We'll be all right."

And they were. USC and the Irish ended that contest in a 21-21 deadlock.

Former Notre Dame sports information director Roger Valdiserri knew both players well.

"Theismann was more of a riverboat gambler. He led the parade. He was like the Pied Piper who always said, 'Follow me.' Montana was more like Cool Hand Luke. He's the guy you would picture at high noon with his hand on the trigger. When he walked on the field, you had the feeing that everything was all right."

Parseghian remembers the 1970 game at USC when Theismann broke the all-time Irish record by throwing for 526 yards and completing 33 of 58 passes in a downpour in the Los Angeles Coliseum.

"The most striking thing to me was his ability to come up with the clutch plays under the most adverse conditions. I remember so vividly a game we had against Southern Cal in 1970 during an absolute deluge. You couldn't believe how terrible the field was."

Offered Pagna, "They both seemed to have a sixth sense. They feel pressure without seeing it."

Said Valdiserri, "If you walked into a crowded room, Theismann would be the first person you'd see, and you'd have to find Montana."

CHAPTER 3

A Devine Time

Faust Fodder

Brian Boulac, the famous Notre Dame recruiter who still works at the University running the Joyce Center, was a fixture at Moeller High School and recruited many Moeller players who contributed during the Ara Parseghian and Dan Devine eras.

I called Brian in 1977 and told him that I thought Harry Oliver could play for them. But Brian said that Coach Devine didn't think that Notre Dame was going to recruit a kicker that year.

So I called Coach Devine myself and I told him that if he had a scholarship available at the end of recruiting season, Harry Oliver would be an excellent choice for a scholarship because I felt he was an outstanding kicker.

Before recruiting ended, they knew they were going to have a scholarship available. Brian called and offered Harry a scholarship and Harry accepted. So Harry went on to Notre Dame.

In 1980 I was still coaching at Moeller, and we were on a trip to play McKinley High School in Canton, Ohio. The afternoon of the game, I took the kids to the Pro Football Hall of Fame to walk around. After that we'd go to eat, then go to church before the game.

That afternoon, Notre Dame was playing Michigan. So a bunch of the young men on our team and myself and a couple of coaches, rather than walking around the Hall of Fame, watched the Notre Dame-Michigan game on television in the Hall of Fame building.

At the end of the game, Harry kicked a 51-yard field goal through the uprights to win the game for Notre Dame. All the guys from Moeller that were watching, plus myself, were cheering. Here was a Moeller man winning the game for Notre Dame.

The next Monday, after we beat McKinley, I was in my office and I got a phone call. It was Coach Dan Devine. Coach says, "Coach, I want to thank you for talking me into taking Harry Oliver. You just helped us win the Michigan game."

"Coach, I know," I told him. "We were watching it at the Pro Football Hall of Fame before we played Canton McKinley and we were all rooting for the Fighting Irish."

Harry put it through the uprights and made us feel very proud that a young man from our high school helped Notre Dame win a football game.

✛

Dan Devine: Tough Competitor, Quiet Demeanor

When it came to comparisons, Dan Devine often came off second best. If Irish fans weren't worried that he didn't have the magnetism or charisma of Ara Parseghian, they stressed (in retrospect) that he didn't have the emotionalism of Gerry Faust or the moxie of Lou Holtz.

No matter. All he did was win games. And, all things concerned, no one coaches at Notre Dame or Green Bay—much less both places, as Devine did—without a serious dose of coaching acumen.

Consider that Devine's six seasons with the Irish produced a national championship campaign in 1977, three bowl victories, an average of nearly nine wins per year—and what former Irish athletic director Moose Krause called the greatest comeback in Notre Dame history, the '79 Cotton Bowl win over Houston.

Three successful seasons (and 27 wins) earlier at Arizona State plus 13 seasons and four bowl wins (among 93 overall) at Missouri combined with the exploits in South Bend to earn Devine a spot in the College Football Hall of Fame.

There was no shortage of memorable moments during the Devine years:

• The comeback wins (led by then-sophomore Joe Montana) over North Carolina and Air Force (both on the road) in his first season in '75.

• The famed '77 matchup with USC in which the Irish warmed up in their traditional blue jerseys before trading them for green just before kickoff.

• The one-sided Cotton Bowl triumph over top-rated Texas and Heisman Trophy winner Earl Campbell to cap the championship year in '77.

• The '78 contest at USC that ended the regular season and might have gone down as another of the greatest Irish comebacks had not the Trojans survived another Montana-led rally to kick a field goal with two seconds left.

• A visit to Tokyo for the '79 Mirage Bowl against Miami.

• The '80 win over Michigan on Harry Oliver's game-winning 51-yard field goal at the final buzzer.

• The 7-0 win over Bear Bryant and Alabama in Birmingham to clinch a Sugar Bowl invitation.

Ultimately, Devine announced his resignation in August prior to that '80 season. He surprised most everyone with the news, doing a live shoot from a South Bend television studio at halftime of a Friday night professional football preseason game.

With wife Jo suffering from multiple sclerosis, Devine simply walked away from the game at age 55.

"The whole decision hinged on this. I'd go to work at 7 a.m. and get home at 11 p.m., seven days a week from August through whatever bowl game we went to. The next day I've got to start recruiting and spend the same hours if I'm going to do a decent job. I don't feel the day after the season is over I should take off and be gone for another three months. I love coaching, but I love my wife more."

And Devine learned what every Irish coach has picked up along the way:

"When Ara resigned, I read a story in which he told all about the Notre Dame pressures. I read it with some skepticism, but everything he said now makes sense to me. What I didn't understand six years ago makes sense to me now."

Maybe what he appreciated most were the plaque presented to him and his team after that heartbreaking '78 loss at USC thanking them for never giving up—and another plaque his seniors game him after the final '80 home game.

Vagas Ferguson: In the Land of Giants

When Notre Dame running back Vagas Ferguson played football at Notre Dame, he was anything but a one-man show. Even with all the accolades he accumulated on his way to becoming the all-time best Irish rusher while on the field from 1976-79, he rubbed elbows with lots of other Irish All-Americans from Ross Browner to Ken MacAfee to Luther Bradley to Bob Golic, Dave Huffman and Tim Foley.

That list didn't even include quarterback Joe Montana, who turned out to be fairly accomplished in his own right. And for much of his career, Ferguson shared top billing at running back with backfield mate Jerome Heavens, who actually broke the career rushing record in '78, a year before Ferguson did it.

Ferguson participated, albeit in a losing role, in one of the most prolific battles between running backs ever seen at Notre Dame Stadium. The date was October 20, 1979, and the opponent was USC. On a balmy, breezy, 75-degree day, Ferguson went toe to toe with the Trojans' Charles White in a matchup of two of the best players in the country (White went on to win the '79 Heisman Trophy—Ferguson finished fifth). White came in leading the nation in rushing—Ferguson stood seventh.

Ferguson broke off a 79-yard run in the first period, only to see the drive stall when the Irish couldn't convert on either third or fourth down from the Trojan one. He later scored on a one-yard dive off right guard for Notre Dame's only first-half touchdown.

By halftime in a 7-7 contest, Ferguson already had 16 rushes for 133 yards, while White had 19 of USC's 22 ground attempts for 110 yards of his own.

And that was only the beginning.

White's two short TD runs in the third period were countered by a 21-yard scoring run by Ferguson late in the third period to make it 21-14 for USC, but the Irish as a group simply didn't have enough firepower.

Ferguson finished with the third highest individual-game rushing total in his career, with 25 carries for 185 yards and a pair of scores. Meanwhile, White finished with 44 attempts (still the most ever against the Irish) for 261 yards and four TDs. Fourth-ranked USC (a 21-21 tie with Stanford the previous Saturday had knocked the Trojans out of the top spot in the polls after 13 consecutive wins) had 591 total yards; ninth-rated Notre Dame had 535 in the 42-23 Trojan victory.

Said USC coach John Robinson of the two backs: "I refuse to compare two great football players. But Charles White is the best football player I've ever been around."

On the same day Ferguson surpassed Heavens to become Notre Dame's all-time leading rusher, White moved into third place on the all-time NCAA rushing chart behind Tony Dorsett and Archie Griffin.

By football standards, it ranked as a shootout at the OK Corral.

Coverboy Career

There was no shortage of high points for Vagas Ferguson in a star-studded career:

- He made the cover of *Sports Illustrated* after the '79 Irish win at Michigan.
- In addition to setting the career rushing mark with 3,472 yards, his 1,437 yards in '79 compose the still-standing single-season record total—and his single-game high of 255 versus Georgia Tech in '79 stood until Julius Jones broke it in 2003.
- He finished with 12 career 100-yard games and ended his Irish career with 13 different game, season and career records.
- As a sophomore in '77, he ran for 100 yards and scored three touchdowns (overshadowing Heisman winner Earl

Campbell in the process) in the Cotton Bowl win over top-ranked Texas that boosted Notre Dame to the national title.

• His senior season technically didn't end with a postseason bowl game, but the Irish finished '79 in Tokyo against Miami of Florida in the Mirage Bowl. Japanese fans may not have known everyone on the Irish roster, but they knew Vagas and he received matinee-idol treatment all week. He didn't disappoint when game time came around—finishing with 35 carries for 177 yards and three scores.

• His first start—and 107 rushing yards that went with it—came in his freshman season in a 21-18 win over Alabama.

Originally from Richmond, Indiana, Ferguson—a first-round NFL draft pick of the New England Patriots—went on to earn a master's degree in education from Miami of Ohio and returned to Richmond High School, his alma mater, as its athletic director and later assistant principal.

Looking back, Ferguson says, "I don't think about all the touchdowns or all the records. I think about what it [Notre Dame] means and what it stands for and I try to live that."

Ferguson remembers being more concerned about academics than football during the recruiting process: "What are they going to do for you, if you can't produce? That eliminated a lot of schools."

When Ferguson was through at Notre Dame, his hometown threw a banquet in his honor. "I would have pushed a peanut all the way here with my nose. Nothing could have kept me from coming here," said Irish coach Dan Devine.

Rusty Lisch:
An Unsung Irish Quarterback

At Notre Dame, where ESPN's Beano Cook predicted multiple Heisman Trophies for Ron Powlus, it's hard to figure how any Notre Dame quarterback could qualify as an unknown.

The position seems to receive as much scrutiny and attention as any in college football, thanks in great part to the past exploits of names like Angelo Bertelli, John Lujack, John Huarte, Terry Hanratty, Joe Theismann, Tom Clements and so many more.

Enter Rusty Lisch.

Lisch earned the distinction of being the Notre Dame quarterback both before and after Joe Montana. The Belleville, Illinois, product began what turned out to be the 1977 national championship season as the Irish regular. He started the Purdue game that year, was replaced by Gary Forystek, returned to the field when Forystek suffered a neck injury, then gave way to Montana in the second half of the pivotal Irish comeback triumph.

Montana played the rest of the way in '77, then all of 1978. Lisch, who didn't play a down in '78, then returned as the starter as a fifth-year player (he was in a five-year architecture program) in '79. He threw for 1,781 yards that year (including 336 in a win over South Carolina and 286 versus USC) while completing 52 percent of his passes overall.

Yet there were legions of Irish fans who wouldn't have recognized his voice. Admittedly media-shy, Lisch wasted no time evacuating the locker room after games. He loved to play golf, was good at it—and after home games often would be playing on the nearby Notre Dame Burke Memorial course while some of his teammates were still being interviewed in the locker room. A Lisch publicity photo sheet distributed by the Notre Dame sports information office included a shot of him putting while wearing sandals.

"I don't clear out quickly to be rude. Having all those people around is a little distracting—I guess you could say I'm a little shy—and I just like to get away from everything after a game," he said.

"I know my position is billed that way, but my goal in life is not to see how much newsprint I can get. When people use football to gain popularity, it is very distressing to me."

As good as he was in football—not to mention golf—those might not have been his best sports. A one-time honorable mention All-State prep basketball player, Lisch carved out a legendary résumé in Notre Dame's famed all-campus Bookstore Basketball Tournament, back in the days when the presence of both varsity football and basketball players made the competition particularly fierce.

In the spring of 1977, Lisch played on the Bookstore runner-up team (interestingly enough, Montana, fellow footballer John Dubenetzky and basketball captain Dave Batton played on the championship unit). Then he played on the winning teams for three straight years from '78 through '80—teaming with varsity basketball players Jeff Carpenter in '78 and Bill Hanzlik in '80.

On one occasion when Lisch's team was slated to play in the final game, a Bookstore commissioner drove to the architecture building minutes before tipoff and found Lisch in the basement. Engrossed in an architecture project, Lisch had forgotten about his team's date in the championship.

Good enough to play in the NFL for the St. Louis Cardinals and Chicago Bears, Lisch always credited his strong faith in God for any of his success. And he never lost his sense of humor.

Asked by *Sports Illustrated* for his reaction to Montana becoming the starter in '77, Lisch said, "I learned a lot."

And, specifically, what?

"That I wasn't as good as Montana."

Later, a teammate was ready to take to the stands to go after a fan who had yelled some unkind remarks about Lisch.

Lisch's reaction? "Don't bother, it was probably my father."

Jerome Heavens:
History Lessons Required

When standout running back Jerome Heavens came from Assumption High School in East St. Louis, Illinois, to Notre Dame to play running back, he wasn't necessarily an expert on the legends of the Four Horsemen, George Gipp and the other larger-than-life icons from the pages of the Irish football history book.

But his successes on the gridiron, in particular the fact that he broke the Notre Dame career rushing record that had stood for 58 years, necessitated that he become familiar with the Gipp story.

After leading the team in rushing as a freshman in 1975 (with 756 yards, most ever by an Irish freshman) and again as a junior in '77 (994 yards) on the Notre Dame championship squad, it slowly but surely became apparent that Gipp's all-time mark of 2,341 rushing yards—that had stood since Gipp's final season in 1920—was in jeopardy.

And as Heavens's productivity enabled him to approach those totals, the questions about Gipp came fast and furious.

Jerome actually remembered attending a Notre Dame home game in 1974 while he was being recruited and having his father point out to him that he could play for the Irish and end up with his name up near Gipp's on the rushing chart.

Jerome didn't necessarily think that much about the record itself as much as about the longevity and consistency that marked its achievement—and the ability of that record to withstand the test of time. As it turned out, Heavens played his way into the backfield quickly enough as a rookie to give himself a chance to break it. It all worked out, despite a sophomore knee injury that limited him to 204 yards in '76.

The record fell five games into his senior season of 1978, thanks to a 120-yard effort in a 26-17 comeback victory over ninth-rated Pittsburgh at Notre Dame Stadium.

"I was tickled by some of the questions the writers asked me. They directed questions to me like I'd been a close friend of Gipp's," said Heavens with a laugh.

"I didn't know him personally, but I've heard that George Gipp was a great individual as well as a great football player."

"The Gipper would have approved of this himself. You don't find a football player with more class than Jerome Heavens," said Irish defensive line coach Joe Yonto.

Heavens actually would have become one of the rare Irish 1,000-yard rushers in '77, but a six-yard loss on his final carry from scrimmage knocked him back to 944 from the 1,000-yard mark. He also became the first Notre Dame player to hit 200 yards in a game, making that figure on the nose against Army in 1978 (that effort broke a 29-year-old record).

Listed as a fullback at 209 pounds, his comparative speed enabled him to play side by side with Vagas Ferguson much of their careers. He ended up the leading Irish rusher—with 22 attempts for 101 yards—in the '78 Cotton Bowl win over top-rated Texas, a victory that vaulted the Irish to the top slot in the final polls.

Dave Huffman:
No Dummy, On or Off Field

Notre Dame center Dave Huffman, a near consensus All-America center for Notre Dame in 1978, was smart enough to know that playing in the middle of the offensive line is no easy way to make headlines no matter how good you are.

So Huffman took matters into his own hands. He wore bright red armbands on his elbows, the easier for Mom to pick you out of a crowd, whether watching in person or on television.

"I wrote, 'Love, Mom,' on them. It wore off after the first couple of practices, but the thought was still there," he said.

"I'm a coward at heart and I go under a lot of people. She likes to know where I'm at."

An anthropology major from Dallas, Huffman proved to be a glib interview prospect for visiting journalists. Here are a few of his witticisms:

• On spending part of a summer researching northeast Indiana's past along the Kankakee River: "It's like looking for King Tut, or the American equivalent. I got right down into it with my trowels, teaspoons and toothbrushes."

• On spending part of the same summer working in a liquor store: "I haven't met many Irishmen on the football team, but I met a lot on that job."

• On being recruited by Texas: "I was interested in that fine school in Austin, but I thought I owed it to myself to get out of the state instead of going where everybody I'd meet would be from El Paso or Sweetwater or Magnolia Tree or Frogs Know or whatever. So I thought I was coming to the big city—and got South Bend."

• On hearing from his home-state acquaintances after Notre Dame beat Texas in the '78 Cotton Bowl: "Like letters that read, 'Come home and we'll kill you. Love from all your buddies.'"

• On his early aspirations: "When I was in high school, my big goal was to play at North Texas State. I was surprised when I was recruited by the big boys."

• On how a Texan ended up in South Bend: "I don't know how I got here. It's cold. The people talk funny. My brother Tim is the only one around here who talks like a human being."

• On running from the huddle to the line of scrimmage: "It keeps things moving and it gets the other team thinking, 'What's this crazy guy going to do next?'"

• On his size 15 feet: "Throw in my brothers and we could row crew using the shoes we have."

Defensive back Dave Duerson (23) soars to break up a pass attempt. Duerson, who played under Dan Devine and Gerry Faust, has returned to campus often in recent years. He is a member of Notre Dame's board of trustees and also serves as current president of the Notre Dame Monogram Club.

• On grabbing the microphone from newly promoted quarterback Joe Montana at a Dillon Hall pep rally on campus early in the '77 season: "Joe feels more at ease when I'm in front of him like this."

• On his goals: "Wouldn't you want to be the first football player ever to play a perfect game?"

• On his placement snapping skills: "One time in practice a play was called for the first count. I thought it was on the second. A coach came running in yelling, 'Why didn't you snap it?' I just told him I didn't want to part with the ball."

• On the team's start in '77: "We had this great idea that we were great and powerful. And then at Mississippi we got our jocks knocked off. We realized our preseason reputation didn't mean beans. We were just another team. We watched films of the Mississippi game. The offense watched our defense. The defense watched our offense. We all saw how we stunk up the place."

• On a conversation he had with a youngster from his hometown about pregame rituals: "I told the poor guy that before every game, I went out and cut a chicken's head off and buried it in front of the Golden Dome. I felt so bad that he believed me and let it go."

Dan Ruettiger: Ultimate Story of Walk-On Makes Good

Notre Dame football is loaded with stories of walk-ons.

Some never played a second in a varsity game, toiling day to day on the prep teams in practice and making their contributions while masquerading as stars of the upcoming Irish opponents.

Others, like Mike Oriard, became starters and captains of Irish teams (Oriard was a senior co-captain and center in 1969).

Then there's Dan Ruettiger.

A spunky but small (5'6 1/2", 184 pounds) defensive end, Ruettiger came from Joliet Catholic (Illinois) High School, determined to find his way to Notre Dame. He originally attended Rockport College on a baseball-wrestling scholarship, worked as a turbine operator at Commonwealth Edison, spent two years in the navy, and then attended Holy Cross College, just across the highway from Notre Dame. He finally was admitted to Notre Dame and attained his goal of qualifying as a walk-on member of the football squad for coaches Ara Parseghian and Dan Devine.

At age 27, Ruettiger actually had his one moment of glory in Notre Dame Stadium in a 1975 game against Georgia Tech in which he played 27 seconds and sacked the Tech quarterback on the final play from scrimmage. His teammates carried him off the field, and the following spring he graduated with a degree in sociology. His identity was questionable enough back then that the individual now known as Rudy was referred to as Ruetty in one newspaper story.

Said Irish star defensive lineman Willie Fry: "Basically, you had to like Rudy because you couldn't get rid of him."

But that was only the start of the story.

Convinced that his journey from Joliet to South Bend was worth something, Ruettiger put together his own film and set out to be a motivational speaker. Sheer determination and peskiness earned him a meeting with screenwriter Angelo Pizzo, who helped create the 1986 hit *Hoosiers*. He literally showed up on Pizzo's Los Angeles doorstep and wouldn't take no for an answer. His persistence won out in the college admissions office, on the football field—and in Hollywood.

Ultimately, Tri-Star Pictures filmed Rudy's story in the first movie shot on the Notre Dame campus since *Knute Rockne, All-American* in 1940. The $15 million project involved actually filming at halftime of the Notre Dame-Boston College game in 1992, with Sean Astin playing Ruettiger. The movie debuted in the fall of 1993 and dovetailed in another career for Ruettiger that has involved motivational speaking, books, tapes, and a foundation.

"Most of my life I was a failure, or so I was told. I stopped listening to people tell me I couldn't make it," he said.

Maybe the most memorable line of the film came when the Notre Dame Stadium groundskeeper tells a despondent Rudy, "You're five feet nothin,' one hundred and nothin,' and you have nearly a speck of athletic ability. And you hung in there with the best college football team in the land for two years. And you're getting a degree from the University of Notre Dame. In this life, you don't have to prove nothin' to nobody but yourself."

Mark Bavaro: One Tough Warrior

The first effort by Notre Dame assistant sports information director Jim Daves to write a feature on Notre Dame senior tight end Mark Bavaro turned out to be a dud.

What Daves learned quickly was that Bavaro—who was originally recruited by Dan Devine and his staff but ended up playing his four seasons under Gerry Faust—chose to let his actions on the field speak for themselves. He was never particularly comfortable in the spotlight. To this day, his file in the Irish publicity archives contains all of three legitimate feature pieces written during his time on campus.

As Bavaro once said during a Super Bowl press conference while he wore a New York Giants uniform, "I don't like reporters because I don't like seeing what I say in the papers."

Bavaro's off-the-field reticence didn't produce much in the way of compelling prose for Daves based on any of the Danvers, Massachusetts, product's comments. So Daves turned to Bavaro's teammates for help. They had plenty to say:

- "There's no pretense. What you see is what you get. All he cares about is winning in the worst way," said Irish receiver coach Mike Stock.

- "I've seen a lot of plays where [tailback] Allen Pinkett would go around on a sweep and pick up big yardage because Bavaro had wiped out the cornerback. I'd hate to be a cornerback and go up against him. I'd just hate it," said Irish strength coach Gary Weil.

- "When I think about a tight end, I think of someone like Bavaro. He's probably the strongest person I've ever worked with or been associated with. He's a gamer. Put that blue jersey on him and he's ready to go," said Weil.

- "Too many receivers think the ball's too heavy once they get it and just fall down. Not Mark. He just tucks it away and goes," said Irish defensive line coach Joe Yonto.

• "He's his own man. He might not talk a lot, but he's still a great one. He can really play ball," said Irish classmate Mike Golic.

Bavaro played behind All-Star Tony Hunter during his freshman year, then missed all but three minutes of his sophomore campaign in '82 with a hand injury. He came into his own as a junior, then led the Irish in receptions as a senior (with 32, four more than then-freshman Tim Brown) while earning first-team Associated Press All-America honors. Despite having a year of eligibility remaining, he opted to move on after graduation and became a fourth-round pick of the Giants.

Quickly nicknamed Rambo as a rookie ("I don't think they could have nicknamed him better," said Irish head coach Gerry Faust), Bavaro claimed two Super Bowl champion rings with the Giants while winning All-Pro honors. That shouldn't have come as a surprise considering his father Anthony once played for the 49ers.

Off the field, Bavaro befriended a New Jersey youth afflicted with a rare form of bone cancer when he learned of the young man's interest in the Giants and Bavaro. Mark once flew from his home in Boston to visit Glenn Siegel, then turned around and flew back.

Bavaro was no more interested in talking about that then he was his football prowess.

Faust recalled Bavaro's ability to dismiss injuries: "He plays with pain better that any football player I've seen in my 37 years of coaching. When he tells you he can't practice, he can't practice. He had a turf knee injury one time against Navy at Giants Stadium and should have missed four weeks. He told me he'd be ready for Penn State two weeks later and he lined up and played the whole game and played excellent. The doctors had said there was no way he'd be ready."

As Daves found out, there's Pulitzer Price-winning material to be found about Mark Bavaro. It just wasn't going to come from the All-Star tight end himself.

CHAPTER 4

Faust Start, Frustrating Finish

Faust Fodder

My tenure at Notre Dame, from the beginning to the end, was always filled with great emotions.

From sky-high hopes in 1981 to hail and farewell in 1985, it was a rapid-fire blend of laughter and tears, triggered by magic moments and discouraging defeats. I felt when we won, the credit should go to the players and assistant coaches. And when we lost, it was my responsibility to carry that burden.

I knew what came along with the title of head coach at Notre Dame. It was something I'd been preparing and praying for since I was a kid, growing up as the son of a renowned high school football coach, Fuzzy Faust, in Dayton, Ohio. Family and religion have always been in the center of my life, although there is room for other lifelong passions. Football is one of them, in particular Notre Dame football.

"Make no little plans," was the watchword for architect Daniel Burnham, the man whose vision helped

My tenure at Notre Dame was always filled with great emotion.

build Chicago into one of the world's most majestic cities. From my earliest days, I was that sort of true believer, dreaming no little dreams. Like a lot of kids around the country, including my coauthor Bob Logan, I grew up listening to the rousing, real-life drama of Irish football on the radio. Unlike the others, I transformed that early love affair into my Golden Dream, the title of the book I coauthored to tell the story of five eventful coaching seasons in the shadow of the Golden Dome.

A Mixed Blessing

Years later, I look back on my adventure with a mixture of gratitude and regret. I still love the lore and legend of Notre Dame as I did on the day I walked to the podium to meet the media after being named the successor to Dan Devine. Time has softened, although not entirely erased, the sadness I felt about not being able to mold the Irish into a top ten team.

Regardless, the invisible mystique that's somehow tangible on every stroll across Notre Dame's bustling campus casts a spell on students and visitors alike. Nobody savors it more than I.

Lou Holtz and I were talking when he was the coach here, and the subject got around to what that mystique is, and how it seems to get stronger with the passing years. Hundreds of reporters and media people kept asking me about it. I always told them it was a special feeling that can't be explained. Lou agreed with me.

I miss coaching since leaving the profession, but I keep coming back to Notre Dame on football weekends. It gives me time to reflect on the wonderful tradition I was lucky enough to be part of.

Knute Rockne was the man who gave us that legacy. When Coach Rockne died in an airplane crash in 1931, they found him with a rosary in his hands. The coaches, the priests and brothers of the Holy Cross order and the people who teach and work at Notre Dame want to carry on Rockne's work, because they love Notre Dame and the Lady on the Golden Dome.

An Unforgettable Spectacle

For me, along with many of the thousands who pack Notre Dame Stadium for home games, the pageantry of a football weekend reinforces and renews the Irish spirit. Walking the campus, I enjoy a nonstop round of handshaking, back-slapping, hugging and greeting people to pause for a nostalgic moment just before the opening kickoff. Sometimes I carry on simultaneous conversations while enjoying the high-stepping entrance of the Irish Guards, followed by cheerleaders, flags and the marching band, but one sight draws my full attention.

When coach Tyrone Willingham sprints out of the tunnel, leading the Irish football team to the sidelines, it brings back a flood of memories of my time coming out into Notre Dame Stadium. A glimpse of sunlight glinting off those gold helmets, worn by players with matching pants and blue jerseys, triggers a wide range of emotions.

Along with the Grotto, the Basilica, Touchdown Jesus and the other symbols of Our Lady's university—especially the young people who come here to earn their degree—that moment always reminds me why Notre Dame is a special place.

The Name of the Game

But once the whistle blows and the game begins, symbolism takes a back seat to reality. Just like the fortunate thousands in the stands, I can sense why those millions of Notre Dame rooters across the country and around the world are plugged into every play. The Irish tradition was built on winning teams, and its legendary players, including seven Heisman Trophy recipients, are acclaimed more for 11 national championships than they are for individual feats.

Sportswriters were only doing their job when they pointed out that my record (30-26-1) fell short of expectations for Notre Dame coaches. Moeller High School in Cincinnati was my first love, and I treasure the success (174-17-2) we had there for 18 years. But my love for Notre Dame is still at the top.

Elation to Deflation

It could have been my first two games as Notre Dame's head coach that proved to be an eerily accurate roadmap for the rocky road I started traveling in the 1981 season with a carload of high hopes. Certainly, the nerve-wracking transition from "What fun!" to "What next?" in just seven days was a traumatic trip for me, my family and our wide circle of friends. Ditto for Notre Dame fans, all anxious to share the boundless optimism I had for Notre Dame

A Day to Remember

If there was a day that we could pick to be frozen in time, chances are it would be September 12, 1981, the steamy afternoon when my fourth-ranked Irish welcomed LSU to Notre Dame Stadium. It was a memorable beginning to the season and to my mercurial sojourn under the Golden Dome.

Expectations for the team already were somewhere in the stratosphere, although what happened in this debut rocketed them into orbit.

Before the first game, I visited several of the Notre Dame students in their dorms. I got the idea after Paul Kollman, a Moeller High graduate who was attending Notre Dame when I was hired—and now Father Paul Kollman, C.S.C.—asked me to speak to the students in Morrissey Hall, where Paul resided. So the preseason buildup kept getting bigger. The Friday night pep rally before the LSU game turned into such a mob scene that it had to be moved outdoors. Electricity was in the air, and it made the unusually warm temperatures seem even hotter as the kickoff drew nearer. The Irish players caught the fever, dominating the LSU Tigers for a convincing 27-9 victory. The elation in the stadium seemed to signify a new era for Notre Dame football.

Irish Talent Farm

David Condon, longtime *Chicago Tribune* columnist and Notre Dame watcher, remarked that I reacted to the victory with the same emotion I displayed at Cincinnati's Moeller High School, "Notre Dame's triple-A farm club." That was a reference to the steady stream of talent we had steered to the Irish in almost two

Bob Crable, a star linebacker for me at Moeller and at Notre Dame, went on to become the head football coach at Moeller.

decades of Moeller's unprecedented domination of Ohio prep football. One of them was All-America linebacker Bob Crable, a 1981 co-captain with Phil Carter.

While the Notre Dame Victory March bounced off the dressing room walls after our LSU victory—it was a parting salute from the Irish band—I remarked,

"They're playing our song." The credit for the victory went to the Irish student section in the stands and our football team.

A football team is only as good as the student body. I'd never seen anything like these students. I expected a tremendous reaction from them, but when we came out of the tunnel, it was unbelievable.

The only other game I had seen in Notre Dame Stadium was in 1952, a 9-0 Irish victory over USC. Not knowing what to expect 29 years later, I borrowed a golf cart and Col. Jack Stephens, the assistant AD, drove me around the campus a few hours before the kickoff to see the mounting excitement so I could tell recruits what it's like on game day at Notre Dame.

Moeller Marauders

While Irish fans bellowed "Ger-ree! Ger-ree!" throughout the 27-9 romp over LSU, our former Moeller High players staged a reunion on the field. Bob Crable, Tim Koegel, Tony Hunter, Rick Naylor, Dave Condini, Harry Oliver, Mark Brooks, Mike Larkin and Mike Lane all played major roles in the Irish victory.

"I think I saw Coach Faust cry about five times today," said Hunter.

"It was his biggest day in coaching," added Koegel. "His excitement rubbed off on us. But we're not thinking about the good old days at Moeller anymore. This was a day for Notre Dame and Gerry Faust."

Linebacker Mike Larkin, who I also coached at Moeller in Cincinnati, and I talk it over on the Irish sideline.

A Short Honeymoon

The Irish zoomed up to No. 1 in the weekly polls before they moved on to the next test at Michigan.

Somehow, the same band of Fighting Irishmen that had spanked LSU soundly failed to show up in the Big House. The Wolverines won handily, 25-7, abruptly ending the euphoria that had Notre Dame fans dreaming of a national championship in 1981. Many people felt this was the turning point of my career at Notre Dame.

In the first quarter, with no score, it was fourth down and we were on the Wolverines' three-yard line. We had noticed watching film that the Michigan team was in man coverage with a full rush to block extra points and field goals. I decided it would be a perfect time to fake a field goal.

We snapped the ball. Tony Hunter, a wingback on our right side of the formation, came across the formation into the flat on the left side. He was wide open, but the rusher from the left side came in fast and our holder was not tall enough to throw over the head of the rusher. So he threw it high and Tony went up for it, making an unbelievable catch. But Tony lost his balance doing so and fell two yards short of the score. It failed and the writers called it a "high school play." If it worked—like it almost did—they would have called it a great, well-designed play.

It was a disappointing afternoon for Notre Dame, my family and myself. Bob Verdi, a worthy successor to the legendary David Condon as the *Chicago Tribune's* ace sports columnist, stuck around after the cheering stopped to discover some of the inner strength that carried my family through the trying times that lay ahead.

"They warned me there would be days like this," I told Verdi. "I told my players that if things always went the way we want them to, if life always was a smooth trip, there would be no reason for eternity. When things go wrong, you have to pick up the pieces and start over again."

Father Knows Best

Though I was very disappointed, I stepped effortlessly into the role of consoling parent when my downcast sons, Gerry, 14, and Steve, 13, entered the nearly deserted Notre Dame dressing room. They were on the verge of tears. I put my arms around them, spoke softly, and the crying stopped. When the three of us left the locker room, my wife, Marlene, and daughter, Julie, were waiting outside. It was an instant replay.

"They take it so hard," I told reporters that day. "I have to tell my players to establish their priorities, and that's what I told my family. This is not the end of the world. It's only one game."

Amid the gathering dusk on September 19, the eve of autumn in 1981, I had to test my memory to recall the last defeat of a team that I coached.

It was 1977. Our Moeller High team lost 13-12 with one second left on a field goal that bounced over the horizontal bar of the uprights. And the last time we were out of a game in the fourth quarter might have been back in 1967 when we lost 40-0. That was our worst defeat at Moeller. But we rebounded and lost only once to that team the remaining 12 seasons that I coached at Moeller.

A Winning Attitude

Bob Logan says that the reason why I am still a welcome visitor on the Notre Dame campus is that I carry the attribute of an unshakable spirit. No matter what I— like any other Notre Dame football coach—have been through, I've always been blessed with the resiliency to bounce back and a love for what Notre Dame stands for.

God has blessed me with the ability to express these feelings to others. The spirit and mystique of the Notre Dame players and coaches, past and present, has created college football's most storied program. I'm proud to have been a small part of that.

Thank You, Lou

I try to get my point across with a good-natured, often self-deprecating style of humor. I took each one of my 26 defeats personally and still replay many of them in my mind. But I found a way to put the situation in perspective. When Lou Holtz came back to Notre Dame for a brief appearance on April 8, 1997, I was asked if I would be one of the speakers to honor Lou for a charity. I was ready with a lighthearted comparison of our coaching résumés: Holtz (1986-96), 100-30-2; Faust (1981-85), 30-26-1.

"Lou and I have been good friends for many years," I told an appreciative audience. "Leaving Notre Dame was tough for me. Many times in newspapers, I read that Gerry Faust was the losingest coach in Notre Dame history. My winning percentage [.535] wasn't the worst, but I know I lost 26 games more than any [previous] coach here.

"My friend Lou finally took this distinction away from me. I just want to ask him one question. Lou, why did you have to make me wait 11 years to break my record? It only took me five years."

I soon switched from a gentle jab to a sentimental salute, spelling out his Lou Holtz tribute this way:

L—Longevity. 132 games, more than any other Notre Dame coach. O—Outstanding. Beat three No. 1 teams: Miami, Colorado, Florida State. U—Ultimate. 1988 national championship. H—Hundred. 100 wins at Notre Dame, second only to Rockne. O—Orchestration. Lou orchestrated a 23-game win streak, tops in Notre Dame history. L—Leader. Irish 79-5-1 when his teams led after three quarters. T—Ten, minus one. He took Notre Dame to nine straight bowl games. Z—Zenith. Tops at turning college football programs around.

Having a Ball—Without the Ball

Losing is an ordeal coaches learn to live with. If they can't, they find another profession. If it happens too often, the fans are not hesitant to supply suggestions about choosing another line of work. That's just another part of the job. Even Penn State's Joe Paterno and Bobby Bowden of Florida State, the twin Godfathers of the collegiate coaching ranks, are not immune from such things in November, the tail end of the season and the time of year when, as one whimsical observer noted, "the frost is on the pumpkin and the blast is on the coach."

Hard enough to take under any circumstances, losing becomes almost unbearable pain when it comes down to a last-second call by an official. There's no instant replay in the college game, so what happens is not always what really happened, but what one of the refs declares really happened. It's a tough situation for the striped-shirt guy who makes the wrong decision, and even more agonizing for the coach whose team gets victimized by the mistake. In pressure-packed situations, the officials can't always be right. A spectacular example of this dilemma, to my dismay, became the notorious phantom USC touchdown with 48 seconds left in our 17-13 loss to the Trojans on November 27, 1982, before a Los Angeles Coliseum throng of 76,459.

Each of my 26 defeats was a gut-wrenching jolt. None of them hurt worse than that four-point loss at USC, because Notre Dame should have been credited with a gallant goal-line stand to preserve a 13-10 victory. Instead, the officials counted the decisive TD when they saw Trojan tailback Michael Harper dive into the end zone. What they didn't see was that Harper was missing some essential baggage in his takeoff across the goal line—the football.

Where was it? Why, in the clutches of Irish defensive end Kevin Griffith at the two-yard line. The stunned players and their bewildered fans were not eased by the picture splashed across the Sunday sports page in the Los Angeles Times. It clearly showed that Harper lost the ball before going airborne.

Revenge Is Sweet and Lengthy

Maybe Lady Luck decided to even the score after plaintive wails of "We wuz robbed" by outraged Irish partisans fell on deaf ears. That controversial setback was Notre Dame's fifth straight in this ferocious rivalry, which began in 1926. The Irish proceeded to topple the Trojans in the next 11 meetings, a streak started in my last three tries (1983-84-85) and continued through the first eight years of the Lou Holtz regime. It got interrupted by a traumatic 17-17 tie in 1994 and grew to a 12-0-1 run the following season before the 1996 Trojans snapped the spell with a 27-20 overtime verdict. That 1982 phantom touchdown still got my goat whenever the topic of conversation turned to USC vs. Notre Dame.

It was John Robinson's last game at USC. He announced his retirement five days before the game. After the game, I went into the locker room and congratulated the USC team for winning their last game for Coach Robinson. They were happy, but I wasn't because our players deserved to have won.

Tim Knows It's Time

Early in my Notre Dame career, Tim Brown admittedly "didn't care about Rockne or the Four Horsemen or any of that stuff." His education about Golden Dome traditions escalated rapidly when we started revving up the team for the annual battle with USC. Along with the customary Xs and Os, game preparations that week included a heaping helping of history.

"Faust would start off by showing us scratchy old films of the first Notre Dame-USC game," Brown recalled. "Then we'd see that USC back [Harper] fumbling before he crossed the goal line. He'd show it to us over and over. At the time, I didn't think much of it."

Brown matured mentally, as well as physically, en route to earning the 1987 Heisman Trophy, becoming the seventh Notre Dame player to win that prize. It was his 56-yard punt return against USC in 1986 that set up John Carney's winning field goal, capping the remarkable fourth-quarter Irish comeback from a 37-20 deficit.

"I've learned to appreciate the rivalry with USC and how it fits into the Notre Dame tradition," Brown said, agreeing that his college experience had prepared him well for pro football and the new opportunities that will arise when his playing days end. "It means a lot to me. I took it for granted then, but now I sometimes pinch myself and realize I was lucky enough to be part of something like that. Coach Faust kept telling us we were fortunate to be there. He was right."

What made my five years at Notre Dame special were all the great young men we recruited, like Tim Brown. I was blessed.

Right Way to Go

After my final game at Notre Dame, a 58-7 loss to Miami on November 30, 1985, some Irish fans berated Hurricanes coach Jimmy Johnson for permitting his players to pile it on in a one-sided game. I had announced my resignation a few days earlier and declined to heave verbal brickbats at the opposing coach. It was a long, hard trek back to Indiana for the weary, frustrated players and coaches, but we did our best to keep everyone on the high road.

Personally, I would put some other kids in there. It's a decision Johnson had to make. He's got to live with himself. I would never knock him. He was going for a national championship, and scores over worthy opponents make a difference.

Bob Logan feels that my lack of malice explains why I have become part of Notre Dame's football tradition, even though my record doesn't rank with Rockne, Leahy or Parseghian.

"He left behind a legacy of all-out effort, sportsmanship and personal responsibility that still stands as a signpost for success to the students who came to the campus after Faust's departure," Logan said. "Add the irrepressible optimism that rubs off on almost everyone he encounters, and it's easy to see why Faust never seems to wear out his welcome under the Golden Dome."

He Can't Fail to Succeed

Reflecting on my five-year struggle to add new chapters to Notre Dame lore, I come face to face with the question I've been asking myself.

To be honest, I don't think I failed. If it all depends on wins and losses, sure, I would have wanted to win a lot more games. But winning happens in a lot of other ways. When you're trying to teach young men and turn them into better men, what they become 10 years down the road is much more important.

I'm very proud of all our players who were at Notre Dame when I was coaching. They are the real winners of Notre Dame football.

What Makes Notre Dame Great?
Its Fans

During the winter of 2004, I was invited to play in a golf outing for a great cause down in Florida. In my cart was one of the country's great football coaches, a gentleman who retired three or four years ago. He built a dynasty and had tremendous success, even earning Coach of the Year honors from the American Football Coaches Association one season.

As we played golf, many sports fans would come up to me and ask for an autograph, to take a picture, or just to shake hands and talk a little bit about Notre Dame. But none recognized my golf companion, this great coach. So I would tell them Coach was with me, and they'd go over and shake his hand or ask for an autograph.

Here I am, I thought to myself, 30-26-1 at Notre Dame. His record far surpasses mine, yet I'm recognized immediately and he isn't. I realized that if he would have been the coach at Notre Dame, he would have received the same kind of attention. Notre Dame is very special. And what makes it special is the Lady on top of the Dome and the great Notre Dame fans.

Spirit and Tradition Never End with a Notre Dame Man

One of the opposing coaches I got to know well while I was at Moeller was Jerry Franks from DeMatha High School in Maryland. Coach Franks had great success there. We played them once, and they came in undefeated. We won the game decisively, but Coach Franks and I became good friends from that.

A couple years after I left Moeller and came to Notre Dame, I received a phone call from a gentleman named Walt Connelly. In those days, colleges were allowed to have birddogs, interested alumni or subway alumni—Walt was a subway alumnus—who looked out for quality student-athletes in their area. Walt said there was a young tight end named Ricky Gray who played at DeMatha and went to Clemson as a freshman, but wasn't happy down there. Ricky was interested in coming to Notre Dame.

So I called Coach Franks. Jerry said Ricky was a quality person and a quality football player with good grades.

"I don't know what can occur at Notre Dame because we don't take transfers here for football," I told Jerry. "Let me check into it." I went to admissions and was told that the only way he would be accepted was if he went to Holy Cross Junior College for a year and continued to keep his good grades. Then he could apply as a student to one of the schools at Notre Dame. But there was no guarantee he would get in.

I called Walt and Jerry back and told them what I'd heard from admissions. I couldn't go to bat for Ricky or anything like that, but his eligibility would be fine. And if Ricky was accepted by Notre Dame, we would honor him with a scholarship. But he'd have to pay his own way to Holy Cross Junior College.

So that's what Ricky did. He paid his own way there and applied to Notre Dame during his spring semester at Holy Cross. He was accepted over the summer. We had one scholarship left and we gave it to him. I had told Ricky that if he got into Notre Dame, it would be very competitive because we had a great tight end there, Mark Bavaro, who we felt had the potential to be an All-American and a pro down the line. Ricky came anyhow.

Ricky played a lot for us as a tight end. We played a lot of two-tight end offense at the time. Ricky had a great career at Notre Dame and graduated with his degree and went back to the Washington, D.C., area.

In 2000, I got a call from Coach Franks. He told me that Ricky was dying of brain cancer. The doctors had operated on him and he was blind. Ricky and his wife Mary had three children, Brian, 12 at the time, Kevin, 8, and Lauren, 4. I started praying for him and called him on the phone one night.

"Rick, I understand that you have terminal cancer," I said.

"Yes, I do," he replied.

"You're a good person. It won't be long and you'll be with God."

"I know that, Coach."

"Ricky, you did three things right in your life."

"What's that, Coach?"

"Number one, you came to Notre Dame. Number two, you became a Catholic. Number three, you married Mary." After I told him that, he just broke up laughing. He thought that was the greatest thing.

"Rick, remember that great pass you caught when we beat LSU down in Louisiana?" I asked.

"Yeah, Coach. But how about that fumble I recovered? That was a key to the game, too."

"You know Rick, I forgot all about that," I said. He started laughing. "That's right, you did recover that fumble. That and the pass you caught were two key points in us upsetting LSU 30-20 down at LSU.

"Rick, I'm not going to keep you, because I know you're not feeling good. But I'll tell you this. When God decides to take you with Him, the players and coaches will get together and raise money for your children so they can go to Catholic high schools.

"Coach, their college is taken care of with insurance policies, but if you could do that for high school, that would be great.

Ricky died a week or so later. I didn't get a chance to go to the funeral, but I wrote a letter to all the players. Father Jim Riehle was involved with it, as was Larry Williams, one of Ricky's teammates who checked everything over for tax deductions for the family. At DeMatha High school, Tom Ponton, their director of development, helped too.

Out of about 140 players Ricky played with, we heard back from more than half of them. The response was unbelievable. And the players called and wrote Mary to give her support and share stories about Ricky. Some went to the funeral. It was just a great outpouring towards a great family. We raised a good amount to help his kids go through the Catholic high schools out there.

Later on, I got the greatest letter back from Mary. She told me how much the letters and support from Ricky's former teammates meant to her and the children. She told me how each of the children was doing. Kevin, the middle child, inherited his father's athletic gift and has excelled in football, baseball and basketball. And she included a few of the letters that our former players wrote to her after Ricky died.

The young men I coached at Notre Dame won more than they lost. But more importantly, they've always been winners off the field.

✝

CHAPTER 5

My Dream Didn't Last

Faust Fodder

One of the reasons my dream didn't last was because I wasn't demanding enough of our players. If I would have demanded more from them, like I did at Moeller, we would have won more. I just felt that, at the college level, the players are more mature—which they are. But demanding that each player give total effort on each and every play is necessary, and I didn't do that. It was a big mistake on my part, and I apologize to our players and our fans.

Everybody's Pal

Above all, of course, the coach has to win and keep winning enough to be in contention almost every season for a major postseason bowl jackpot.

Understandably, much of in-season life becomes an exhausting treadmill of meetings with assistants, rerunning game film, endless preparation, leading up to the weekly trial by fire in stadiums crammed with unforgiving fans. I went through all that, but I just couldn't wall myself off from the friends and the fans and the causes that demanded pieces of my time.

That might have had something to do with my inability to get the Irish over the hump and consistently back into the top 10 weekly rankings that serve as a barometer of coaching success or failure. But while my teams struggled, I dealt with the personal pain, finding time for my legion of friends, young and old, while making new ones. I still have great respect for the Golden Domers. And they welcome me on every visit to the campus and Notre Dame Stadium, living proof that there are exceptions to Leo Durocher's famous quote: "Nice guys finish last."

Losing's Never Fun

Of course, the world has changed dramatically—and traumatically—in the years since I was on the Notre Dame sidelines. One thing hasn't changed. A small percentage of rabid fans always react as though losing a football game is a capital offense. Their methods of venting frustration sometimes border on the sadistic. Even though things didn't go well on the scoreboard, where it matters most, my critics seldom descended to that level.

One reason: I felt the fans' pain. It was crystal clear to even the most vocal of my detractors that I was feeling more pain than they were. I wore my emotions on my sleeve. If optimism ever gets installed as an Olympic

It was clear to even the most vocal of my detractors that I was feel-ing more pain than they were.

sport, I might come home with a bunch of gold medals draped around my neck. My natural tendency to see a turning point somewhere close, any day, kept getting sacked under a pile of injuries, bad breaks and gut-wrenching losses. I was responsible for the fundamental shortcomings of our Notre Dame teams, but I never stopped believing that the mistakes could be corrected and the breakdowns in execution minimized by sheer effort.

Father Jim Riehle:
A Giant Among Notre Dame People

When coaches get caught up in the stress and strain of competition, they seldom find time to be people persons. That reverses the cliché, "You can't see the forest for the trees." In sports, the big picture often crowds out the small stuff, especially the little people. Invitations are ignored, phone calls go unanswered and unopened mail piles up so coaching staffs can cram one more wrinkle into their weekly game plans. It's especially true in big-time college football, where the elite teams undergo nonstop scrutiny and relentless pressure to win—or else.

I went through all of that, and more, during my five years as Notre Dame's head man. In some ways it was even more difficult for me, because the euphoric buildup surrounding my arrival gradually eroded. At a place where winning big has been a habit for generations, not doing so is unacceptable. Regardless of the reasons, Irish fans are not good losers, nor am I. I knew that when I took the job and I did everything I could to live up to their near-impossible expectations.

Somehow, in the midst of that emotional maelstrom, I still found time to reach out to people. One of my closest friends on campus, Father James Riehle, saw that happen over and over, even when Irish fans began grumbling about my lack of success on the field.

Father Jim, our team chaplain for five years as well as chaplain and Notre Dame Monogram Club executive director for years, is one of the great Notre Dame men. He was always there when needed. Players, coaches and coaches' families could always count on Father Riehle to guide them in good times as well as bad times. On gameday mass for the players and coaches, his sermons always pertained to Christ and his teachings, but he always found a way to include a pep talk to the team. His talks could match any of my own or those of Rockne, Holtz, or Parseghian. Even I would come out of the mass ready to play against any opponent.

Atz the Spirit

Father Riehle often tells the story of Brian Atz. At 28, Atz, a lifelong Notre Dame fan, was paralyzed from the neck down in a car accident. Unable to talk, Atz still rooted silently, although just as fervently, for the Irish. When I was told about the situation, I invited Atz to watch his heroes demolish Colorado, 55-14, on September 22, 1984, in Notre Dame Stadium.

Afterwards, we had Atz wheeled into the Irish dressing room, to listen with tear-filled eyes while the players serenaded their faithful fan with a rousing chorus of the Notre Dame Victory March. Then the team presented Atz with the game ball.

"That's how Gerry reaches out to people," Father Riehle said. "He finds a way to share some of his best moments with those who are struggling to overcome personal tragedies."

It's Important to Help Others

I really feel that being the Notre Dame head football coach, you have an obligation to reach out to people. Sometimes it's just a short, fervent pep talk, much like the ones that worked so well for me at Moeller High School, but did not pack the same punch at Notre Dame. Regardless, when somebody needed help, I would try to see them in person or call them. I don't recall all the names or faces, though there are exceptions.

Not long ago, I got a call from a friend telling me that Mark Tupa, a nephew of Tom Tupa, the former Ohio State quarterback and punter who has enjoyed a long, productive NFL career, was paralyzed by a head-on collision in a high school football game. He was undergoing intensive therapy in a Cleveland hospital.

When I went to visit Mark, they told me I couldn't see him. So I gave his parents a copy of *The Golden Dream* and autographed the book to tell him not to give up.

If people refuse to give up, some wonderful things can come out of very difficult situations. I was coaching at Moeller when Paul Silva, a player on the sophomore team, broke his neck in a pileup. I traveled from Cincinnati to Cleveland once every four weeks to see him and encourage him. He kept believing and working until he could walk again. Now Paul's perfectly normal, a bank executive with children of his own.

A Helping Word

I never looked at the sportswriters covering our teams as potential enemies, to be kept at arm's length. We had an open-door policy with the media that probably caused some problems, especially with writers who contrasted my eternal optimism to the paucity of bowl trips for Notre Dame. Even so, that door seldom slammed shut, right up to the day I stepped down in 1985. I understood that they had their job to do.

Some writers admitted that they rooted for us personally, even though newspaper ethics required them to keep mentioning such depressing details as the final score in their Notre Dame game stories.

A Boost for Chris

Years later, Bob Logan told me this story from Bob Becker, the sports editor of the *Grand Rapids* [Michigan] *Press*.

"Bob Becker still shakes his head at the memory of a warm gesture by Faust," Logan said. "He mentioned to the Irish coach that his son, Chris, was a high school student, with the usual concerns of youngsters caught in the 1980s transition from slower-paced, stable Midwestern mores to the MTV generation. Soon after that, Chris starting receiving letters from Coach Faust, offering praise, encouragement and enthusiasm.

"Chris got the letters from Gerry for a couple of years, and he still has them," Becker said. "He couldn't believe that a Notre Dame coach would take the time to keep tabs on how a young fellow's grades were com-

ing along. He was impressed that Faust was concerned about somebody he'd never met. So was I."

Chris is now a successful lawyer.

Pinkett's Perspective

Others, notably outstanding tailback Allen Pinkett, took a philosophical tack amid the turmoil of those times. Since becoming a color commentator with play-by-play veteran Tony Roberts on nationwide radio broadcasts of Notre Dame games, Pinkett is pleased to see that his former coach gets a warm welcome when he backslaps his way through the press box.

"How that man survived what he went through without drinking is something I'll never understand," Pinkett said with a reminiscent grin. "Whenever I see Coach Faust, I get a mental picture of him running up and down our sideline before a crucial third-down play, hollering at everybody, 'Say a Hail Mary!' He got so emotionally wound up, I sometimes worried about him.

"But he loved Notre Dame then and still does. It's a shame we couldn't win more games for him. Coach Faust had to find out the way it is with this team, and so does everybody who walks in the footsteps of Knute Rockne. When we win, the coach doesn't get credit, because it's supposed to happen. If we lose, the coach gets second-guessed from coast to coast."

One of Pinkett's favorite memories was Notre Dame's 19-7 victory over USC on November 24, 1984. It ended a dreary stretch of 18 years, an 0-7-1 run of Trojan domination, since the last Notre Dame triumph in Los Angeles Coliseum. Pinkett ran for 98 yards on the soggy turf, but gladly shared laurels with John Carney, who defied the treacherous footing to boot a pair of 45-

A standout in the backfield for my Notre Dame teams and with the Houston Oilers in the NFL, Allen Pinkett now serves as color commentator with play-by-play veteran Tony Roberts on Notre Dame radio broadcasts.

yard field goals. I was criticized for many of my decisions, but not for choosing to award walk-on Carney a scholarship. Carney holds the all-time Irish record with 51 career field goals, and is still booting NFL three-pointers well into the 21st century.

Faust on Faust

It took time, lots of time, to heal the pain that I underwent when I came to the realization that Notre Dame would be better off with a new football coach. True to their word, Father Ted Hesburgh and Father

Edmund Joyce gave me the full five-year tenure of my contract, but others were calling for my scalp. Years of reflection on how my dream job got derailed by too many nightmarish losses finally brought me full circle, all the way around to the reasons why I'd been unable to translate my coaching wins at Cincinnati's Moeller High School into similar success with the Irish.

At a conservative estimate, upwards of 10,000 other theories on that subject already had been hashed and rehashed by the time Lou Holtz stepped in to replace me and in 1986 took over the football program. I read a few of them, agreed with some of the points they made and disagreed with most of the speculation.

I told Father Joyce, "Notre Dame's been too good to me for this to continue." I tried never to let this team down, but they needed a new coach and a new direction. It was a decision I thought about and prayed about. Things came down to where I was convinced trying to stay on would only cause more problems, because they'd have had to let me go sooner or later.

When we're not winning enough football games, it's tough on everybody. The bottom line is you have to win. We won a lot of big games, but lost some to teams we should have beaten. So it was time for me to go. I love Notre Dame, and I realize I wasn't getting some things done that the football coach here is responsible for doing.

I can't complain about the way I was treated, especially by the press and the Notre Dame people. They were very fair to me, but when a Notre Dame coach has a 30-26-1 record, there's not too many good things to write about or cheer about and I understand that.

How would I sum up my Notre Dame experience?

After 21 years at Moeller, it's my first love, and I go back there every year. Even so, my love for Notre Dame is at the top. The five years I spent there were years of adversity, but they were years of joy. I love Our Lady's university, the Holy Cross order and the tradition of Notre Dame football.

Rock's Still Tops

In between all the ups and downs, there still was time for some light moments in my years at Notre Dame when I started reading newspaper speculation about my prospects for survival.

"I used to tell people I wanted to become the first man to coach at Notre Dame longer than Rockne's 13 years," I said after one of those gloom-and-doom feature stories landed on my desk in the football office. "Maybe I better start following Rock's example and win more football games."

Good News, Bad News

At all major universities, a local car dealer furnishes cars to the coaching staff. My car coach at Notre Dame was Mike Leep of Gurley Leep Automotive Group. Mike was the head of the car program for all of our assistant coaches and myself. Mike always asked me what I wanted. I just asked him for a midsize car. He always gave me a Buick, which was a great car.

One day as I left for a recruiting trip, I drove from Notre Dame out to the South Bend airport. I went to the parking lot to park the car. I was running late and didn't have much time to catch the airplane. All of the sudden, I got hit from the side by an elderly woman. She smashed in the whole right side of the car.

We got out of our cars and she said, "I didn't see the stop sign."

"Ma'am, don't worry about it," I told her.

"Well, I've got insurance," she responded. I told her I had to go before I missed my flight.

"Mike Leep owns this car," I told her as I handed her my card. "He owns Gurley Leep. You just give the insurance number to him."

So I left the keys in the car and headed into the airport. After that, I called Mike.

"Mike," I said. "Do you want the good news first or the bad news?"

"Give me the bad news first," he said.

"The bad news is that the car got wrecked and you have to come over here and pick it up and leave another car for me so I can get back," I said. "The good news is that the woman who hit me has insurance and it was her fault. So your body shop is going to make some money off of redoing the car."

So that night, when I got back, there was a car sitting for me to drive home.

Mike Leep is still a car coach at Notre Dame. He has great love for the university and he's a great person himself. To this day, 24 years later, we're still the best of friends.

Gerry and Digger

My spirits also got a lift from my friendship with Richard "Digger" Phelps, the colorful Irish basketball coach who always showed up before games sporting a green carnation in his buttonhole. We got along from the moment we posed for pictures on the Joyce Athletic and Convocation Center court, and I promptly swished a 30-foot jump shot.

"Say, you'll fit right in around here," the irrepressible Phelps said.

Later, both of us showed up for an Irish track meet and I was handed a starter's pistol to get some sprinters off and running.

"Hey, watch where you're waving that thing," Digger cautioned. "With my luck, you might hit me."

"With my luck, I might miss you," I said.

The Word Gets Out

But the handwriting already was on the wall. It got spelled out in a Chicago newspaper story dissecting what the writer described as three years of failure. Several disgruntled Irish players were quoted in the story, complaining about the way I coached. Their comments quickly spread around the country, and rebuttals by me couldn't repair the damage, even though four of the five players said they were misquoted.

After the last practice before my final game against Miami, I was walking off the field when Phil Hersh came up to me. "Coach," he said, "I really have respect for you. You never said anything to me about the article I wrote two years ago and you always have treated me fairly."

I had no animosity toward Phil, but some things in his article were not the truth. But it was over and I wished him the best in life and told him he was still a friend.

Grace Under Fire

I left Notre Dame without whining, finger-pointing or buck-passing. With one game left in the 1985 season, I called Father Hesburgh to tell him the time had come, then sought out Father Joyce to give him the word in person.

Father Joyce hugged me with tears in his eyes. He told me, "Coach, I was hoping you'd do this." Then the media started coming in from all over the country, and I had to answer their questions for the rest of the day and again that night, when a new batch of reporters arrived.

Hail and Farewell

Dennis Kraft, veteran sports editor of the *Elkhart Truth*, told Bob Logan that my so-long session with the media was unlike anything he'd seen in decades of covering Notre Dame.

"Gerry was calm when he met with us for the last time, but it was easy to tell he'd been under tremendous strain," Kraft said. "The point he wanted to make is that he was doing the best thing for Notre Dame, but we were aware it would be better for him and his family, too. The writers kept asking why his teams didn't perform up to their potential, and he told them the blame belonged to him, not the players.

"Then he said, 'I want you guys to know I have no animosity toward any of you. I'd like to remain friends, and I'll be glad to talk things over whenever we meet again.' When Gerry walked out, there was dead silence in the room for a few minutes."

Joe Doyle, sports editor emeritus of the *South Bend Tribune*, has seen Notre Dame coaches of all sizes, shapes and temperaments come and go in half a century on the Irish beat. He, too, thought that I was one of a kind.

"Maybe Gerry was too nice a guy to chop off some heads when he should have," Doyle noted. "But a lot of Notre Dame people figured that it was just too big a jump from high school coaching into this kind of hot seat."

Best of Friends

In 1980, when I became the 24th head football coach at the University of Notre Dame, I became acquainted with many, many people. To this day, I have great friendships with almost 95 percent of all the people that I've met.

Frank Eck, Sante Cundari, and Ray Meyo—all three are big Notre Dame fans; Eck and Meyo are graduates and generous supporters of Notre Dame. I have many friends like those three and over the years our friendship has even gotten better. They were always very supportive when I was the coach there.

We always talk year-round about Notre Dame football. To this day, they call me at least once a week. During the season, when things sometimes don't go right, they really get upset and they start letting their emotions go and tell me how they think this and that is wrong.

I respond to them in the same way: "Frank, Sante, Ray, what were you saying when I was coaching there?"

And they'll all shut up and they'll all start laughing. Because, if you're truly a Notre Dame fan, it's from the heart. And when things don't go right, you get upset and you start blaming this and that.

I laugh about it all the time because they're still my best friends to this day. Yet when I was the head coach, they were on my back just like they're on other coaches' backs now, because they have such a great love for Notre Dame.

People from the Past

For several years, each summer I would go on an outing to a Chicago Cubs game with Frank Eck, Paul Mainieri, the baseball coach at Notre Dame, and the Irish hockey coach, Dave Poulin. Frank and I would fly to South Bend and pick up Poulin and Mainieri and then we'd all fly to old Meigs Field on the lakefront in Chicago and take a cab to Wrigley Field. We would meet Jim Hendry, who today is the general manager of the Cubs. We took one of these trips about five years ago when he was the assistant general manager.

There's an irony to this story that goes back to the days I was coaching at Notre Dame. I was in Florida on a recruiting trip and I stopped in Miami to recruit Alonzo Highsmith, who was a great fullback at Christopher Columbus High School in the early 1980s. The head coach at Columbus High came up to me while I was there and said that he had a couple of assistant coaches who also coached baseball and taught at the school and that they would like to meet me, the Notre Dame coach. I said I'd be glad to. I sat down with them for about 20 or 25 minutes. They were two aspiring young teachers and coaches. I was impressed. One of the assistant football coaches I talked to was the head baseball coach at Christopher Columbus, and his name was Jim Hendry. The other was Hendry's assistant baseball coach at the time, and his name was Paul Mainieri.

A few years after our meeting, Hendry made a big jump and become the head baseball coach at Creighton University in Omaha, where he went 282-171-2. Paul moved on to become the head coach at St. Thomas University in Florida at age 24, and later became the first civilian head coach in Air Force history before coming to Notre Dame in 1994. In February, 2003, Hendry came to Notre Dame as the featured speaker at Notre Dame baseball's "Opening Night Dinner." I met both of them when they were starting out, and look what they've done now.

When we go to the Cubs games, we usually sit with Hendry, next to the press box. I have a great love for Wrigley Field and love watching a baseball game there. That afternoon about five years ago, I looked down over the fans in the stands and down to my right near the field was John Heisler—my coauthor on this book and Notre Dame's sports information director—with his assistants Sue McGonigal, Alan Wasielewski, and Bernie Cafarelli. They were at the sports information office outing. The window was open and I yelled down at them. They yelled back up. They were excited to see me and I was excited to see them.

On one little trip every year, I have the opportunity to engage with old friends I either worked with or met when I was at Notre Dame. What a great day it was.

Happy Trails

My post-coaching era has proven that time really does heal wounds. Maybe not all, but most. It's a mutual lovefest when I appear on campus, or wherever dedicated Golden Domers gather. The University showed its gratitude for the way I fought the good fight, bleeding blue at every turn. They surprised me by making me a member of the Notre Dame Monogram Club. Father Riehle and Chuck Lennon had me speak at the Notre Dame Florida Fling and they surprised me with that honor. It was something I always wanted, but never told anyone.

And almost as uplifting to my spirit—as if it needed another boost—was the 2001 NFL Films documentary based on my book, *The Golden Dream.*

I had tears in my eyes watching the program. Most of the film was shot at Notre Dame, and when the producer, Neil Zender, called to tell me it had won an Emmy, the tears came back again. Hopefully, Irish fans don't mind me wearing ND fervor on my sleeve.

It's hard to keep track of all the phone calls, letters and visits and prayers for others. When I was Notre Dame's coach, I couldn't say no, and that was part of the problem. Looking back, I'd have done the same thing over again.

I have no regrets, just a lot of memories, and I thank Our Lord, Our Lady, Father Hesburgh, Father Joyce and the Notre Dame family for allowing me to be one of them for five great years. I was the coach at this great university—Notre Dame.

✛

CHAPTER 6

Holtz, That Tiger

Faust Fodder

While I was the head coach at Notre Dame and Lou Holtz was still at Minnesota, Lou Holtz called me and told me that his son, Skip, was going to Notre Dame and he asked me if I would look out for him. I told Coach Holtz that I'd be more than happy to do that. Skip started off at Holy Cross Junior College across the street from Notre Dame and transferred to Notre Dame in 1984.

Skip liked football and wanted to attend some of the games. So I called Skip up and Skip came over. I always had a sideline pass for him and he would come and always watch the games from the sidelines. After his father became the head coach, Skip joined the team and appeared in 11 games on special teams in 1986.

When I decided to step down as the coach and Lou was named the head football coach at Notre Dame, the first day that he came in as the new head football coach, I sat down with him and Gene Corrigan, the athletic director, for three and a half hours. I told him the differences between Notre Dame and any other school, what you could do and what you couldn't do. I talked to him about the players and the people we were recruiting. I talked to him about staff and everything like that. I answered every question he had.

I tried to be very honest and up front with him so that he could go into the job knowing its strengths and pitfalls. I don't think Coach Holtz has ever forgotten, because two or three times over the past 20 years he's thanked me for that.

Over the first year, when something would come up that he wasn't familiar with, or didn't know why a meeting was being called or what the meeting was about, Lou would always call and ask and I would tell him. I think one of the strong points of Coach Holtz is that if he doesn't know the answer, he's going to try to find the answer out. I think that one of the strengths that he has as a coach is depth of organization.

✛

Winston Churchill probably pegged Lou Holtz as well as anyone could, even if unintentionally.

The British prime minister's description of Russia as "a riddle, inside a mystery, wrapped in an enigma," sounds suspiciously like the man who coached, rejuvenated, and exalted the Notre Dame football team for 11 unforgettable years. About the only adjective that fails to fit the Holtz reign under the Golden Dome would be "boring."

Notre Dame alumni all over the globe, in or out of the subway, got caught up in the fervor of Holtz's drive for perfection from 1986 through 1996. They lived and died with his Fighting Irish, getting handsomely rewarded by 100 victories in

Lou Holtz always demanded maximum effort from his Notre Dame players—and himself.

those 11 seasons. The legend of Lou, right next to Knute Rockne's 105 wins, is as secure as the bricks and mortar of Notre Dame Stadium.

Louis Leo Holtz put a premium on that success. He demanded all his players could give, and those who matched their hard-driving coach's intensity sooner or later learned they were becoming better men, not just better football players. Holtz owned an impressive arsenal of coaching techniques to motivate the Irish, even performing occasional magic tricks to ease the tension on the eve of a big game. Whatever his methods, they translated into real magic for Notre Dame on the gridiron.

He's still best known, of course, for the wry, self-deprecating humor that kept this 155-pound human dynamo "two steps ahead of the posse," to hear him tell it, throughout his coaching career. A glance at the record book proves that Holtz was mainly downplaying his own ability. Most Notre Dame fans, then and now, regard the slender sage with the lisping voice as a coaching genius to equal Hall of Famers Rockne, Frank Leahy and Ara Parseghian.

What is certain is that Holtz picked up the torch of Irish legend and kept it burning for more than a decade. There were ample triumphs and a few tragedies during Holtz's 132-game tenure in South Bend. Rain, shine, or snow, he had a quip for all seasons, cementing his reputation as master of the one-liner, not to mention the offensive and defensive line. Like virtually everything else the coach did, humor was part of his daily game plan.

"Besides," Holtz often added with a disarming grin, "it helps me keep what's left of my sanity."

No Frightening Irish

"I don't believe all that stuff about the ghosts of Notre Dame legends walking around the campus," the late Irish assistant coach and administrator George Kelly once said. "Our mystique was built by real people, like Knute Rockne, Lou Holtz and lots of others. I never saw anybody take losses any harder than Holtz. It wears down every coach, but he had to learn how to deal with them. That's why Lou never tried to build up his team too much after a win. He knew what a fine line there is between that and defeat."

Along with the legendary Moose Krause, Kelly saw the Irish tradition grow for more than three decades as an assistant coach under Ara Parseghian, an athletic department mainstay and a trusted aide to Holtz. Kelly never got too busy to give players a pat on the back, pause to fill in the gaps for writers in search of Notre Dame lore or direct bewildered freshmen to the right place on the sprawling Note Dame campus.

"I love it here, but when I see the pressure on Ara, Lou and the other head coaches, I'm thankful I didn't have to go through that," Kelly reflected. "The expectations of success and the daily demands on them really changed their lives."

No Crying Towels

Through most of his 11 seasons at Notre Dame, Lou Holtz declined frequent invitations to expound on the constant pressure and daily problems of his job.

"There are lots of good reasons why I don't expect any sympathy," Holtz pointed out. "For one thing, most people don't care about my problems and the rest are glad I have them. I'm aware everybody expects Notre Dame to win every game. For our fans, the only thing more important than winning is breathing.

"All opponents regard playing Notre Dame as their big game. I regard that as part of the experience that will help our young men to prepare for success in whatever they do later."

Just Win, Baby

Lou Holtz didn't take long to learn the drill when he took over as Notre Dame's head football coach in 1986.

"Everybody wants Notre Dame to win, including our paperboy," he said. "When we lose a game and I go out to get the newspaper next morning, it's in the bushes instead of on the front porch."

Tough Teacher

"I learned early that discipline is the way to get things done," Holtz recalled of his Catholic grade school days back in Ohio. "Sister Mary Harriet was my teacher, and she was tougher than Bear Bryant. The kids in my class celebrated when we finished her classes. Then we came back to St. Ambrose after summer vacation and found out she was now the principal."

Two Left Feet

For years, Lou Holtz has been one of the nation's most sought-after motivational speakers. The former Notre Dame coach regularly travels to make rousing pep talks to executives, salespeople and various groups all over America. He overcame a speech impediment with therapy, to hold audiences spellbound with the same fiery oratory that inspired his Irish football teams.

"I know how to speak," Holtz said. "Just don't ask me to dance."

No Gator Aid Needed

Holtz began stocking that bottomless barrel of quips early in his coaching career. He termed spring practice at William & Mary, his first head-coaching post, as "no tougher than your average death march." Years later, at Notre Dame, his players were warned they were in for eight hours of practice.

"What I really meant was 8 a.m. to 8 p.m.," he explained.

When Holtz steered Arkansas to an Orange Bowl bid in 1977, ecstatic Razorback fans showered the field with oranges to kick off the celebration. Holtz, always ready to pounce on a good line, didn't miss this opening.

"I'm sure glad we aren't going to the Gator Bowl," he said.

Golden Dreams

If there was a regret for Lou Holtz at Notre Dame it was the way a second national championship eluded his team after winning one when the Irish went 12-0 in 1988 to finish atop the final polls. After moving on to become a college football analyst for CBS-TV and then the head coach at South Carolina, Holtz repeatedly made clear his heart—and eventually the rest of him—will always be at Notre Dame.

"It was only right for Beth to buy cemetery plots for us close to the Lady on the Dome," Holtz said of his wife's plan for their final resting place. "The alumni used to bury me here every Saturday."

Typically, Holtz blamed himself for not boosting Notre Dame's bag of national titles to a dozen or more.

"We became the hunted, because we were trying to maintain our top spot," the coach reflected on the aftermath of 1988. "Instead of getting too comfortable with the view up there, we should have been telling the players they were capable of setting goals, and reaching them, that nobody thought we could make.

The hunger that kept us going [in 1988] faded away. I didn't give them bigger dreams to shoot for."

Regardless, many Irish fans still share Lou's frustration about the 1993 crown that slipped off Irish heads, thanks to a heartbreaking 41-39 upset loss to Boston College, before a stunned Notre Dame Stadium throng viewing the regular-season finale. The fired-up Irish beat Florida State 31-24 in their head-to-head mid-November showdown and both teams finished 12-1, but poll voters awarded the top spot to the Seminoles.

"I came here hoping to be the lucky coach who won three national championships," Holtz reflected after he resigned in 1996. "Instead, I was the unlucky coach who lost three of them."

Woody Wages Total War

Lou Holtz earned his first national championship ring in 1968, as an assistant to Woody Hayes at Ohio State. A ferocious competitor, Hayes never failed to post big numbers, especially against Michigan.

With the Buckeyes en route to a 50-14 rout of their Big Ten rival, Hayes made them go for a two-point conversion after a late-game TD. "Why did you go for two in that spot?" Holtz asked his boss.

"Because they wouldn't let me go for three," Hayes shot back.

"Back in 1971," Holtz recalled. "Bobby Bowden [then coaching at West Virginia] beat my William & Mary team 43-7. We were friends, so I phoned to ask why he ran up the score. He said, 'You coach your team and I'll coach mine. I have an obligation to get my team ready for the rest of the schedule.'"

Holtz got the message.

"Bobby was telling me it was my team's job to hold the score down, not his," he said.

Arnold Who?

Early in his Notre Dame coaching regime, neither Lou Holtz nor actor-turned politician Arnold Schwarzenegger had yet become household names. Regardless, Holtz was kept busy laughing off comparisons between himself and legendary predecessors Knute Rockne, Frank Leahy and Ara Parseghian, mostly by Irish fans with sky-high expectations.

"That would be like comparing me with Arnold Schwartzenheimer, or whatever his name is," Holtz said. "I can't imagine why anyone would think of me as a legend. I wasn't smart enough to be a Notre Dame student or good enough to play football here. The standards for Notre Dame coaches must have come down a lot for them to hire me.

"What I am is a plugger. I look funny and I talk with a lisp. If I can get our players to work on fundamentals and never start thinking they're good enough, I'll be satisfied."

Rosy Relationship

Dick Rosenthal believed in Lou's ability, but not in all of the new Irish coach's snappy one-liners. Rosenthal knew that Holtz intended them as comic relief from the high-intensity grind of collegiate football. It's no laughing matter on the scoreboard, because all coaches know that's the bottom line for their careers.

Holtz and Rosenthal, Notre Dame's athletic director, became close friends. Rosenthal understood that his workaholic coach's blend of high visibility and winning football was a powerful combination, on the field and at the box office. Demand for tickets at Notre Dame Stadium and on the road soared when the quotable coach quickly brought the Irish back to rejoin the nation's elite programs. One of Holtz's lasting legacies was a total overhaul that boosted Notre Dame Stadium's seating capacity to 80,795 from the traditional 59,075.

So Rosenthal was not perturbed by such Holtz routines as the oft-repeated one about finishing 234th out of 278 graduates in his high school class.

"If that's the case, the 233 kids ahead of Lou must have been very impressive," Rosenthal said.

No Football Factory

Holtz soon discovered that things were done differently at Notre Dame than they had been at Minnesota and Arkansas, two earlier rungs on his coaching ladder.

"Any college can put a top 10 team on the field if football is its top priority, 24 hours a day," Holtz said. "Notre Dame is unique. We're expected to win every game, but football is our No. 1 priority three hours a day. The players we recruit do not need NFL careers to be successful in life."

Coaching Springboard

Assistant coaches came and went to and from Notre Dame in a steady stream during the Holtz regime, because the Irish success provided many head coaching and NFL opportunities for Holtz staff members. Holtz realized that stability on Penn State's coaching staff was a crucial ingredient in making Joe Paterno one of the college game's all-time winners in Joe Pa's half-century as the ayatollah of Happy Valley. Holtz learned other valuable lessons from legends like Paterno, Bear Bryant and Bo Schembechler. As a young coach, he invaded the office of Texas coach Darrell Royal to ask 80 questions that became a treasure trove of winning football on pages of scribbled notes that Holtz kept for years.

No wonder Paterno paid him the ultimate tribute after Notre Dame topped the Nittany Lions 21-3 en route to the 1988 national championship: "Lou Holtz is a coaches' coach."

Holtz Helps Helpers

Holtz came up the hard way himself. From a scrawny line-backer at Kent State in Ohio to low-pay, long-hours apprentice-ships at five colleges before his 1969 debut as head man at William & Mary, he paid his dues in the profession. Few understood better than Holtz that timing is crucial in the coaching job market, so he made sure his aides got their chances to move up.

It was painful to say goodbye to Barry Alvarez, the Irish defensive coordinator who played a major role in the all-con-quering 1988 march to the national championship. Yet Holtz knew the window of opportunity at Wisconsin would slam shut if Alvarez hesitated, so after the 1989 season he sent the burly ex-marine off to turn the Badgers into a perennial Big Ten pow-erhouse.

"Barry was ready to be a winning head coach at Wisconsin, even though I hated to lose him," Holtz said. "Any attempt by me to prevent my assistants from advancing would be wrong."

All in the Family

One assistant who could be counted on to stay close to the fold is Skip Holtz, the personable son of the coach. Skip quickly emerged as a media favorite while tutoring the Irish receivers on his dad's staff in 1991-93. The younger Holtz later got his head coaching shot at Connecticut—where Lou served as secondary coach in 1964-65—and moved on to become his dad's top assistant at South Carolina.

For the Holtz family, that father-son coaching reunion afforded more than a new career start. It provided a new lease on life, with Lou's wife Beth Holtz waging a courageous fight against cancer and Skip recovering from a painful abdominal ailment. Once again, Lou Holtz won on and off the field, turning South Carolina into Gamecock country.

During the brief sojourn of Skip Holtz as an Irish assistant, he provided useful insights and lively quotes to fill writers' notebooks. Skip's favorite story was a sure-fire hit with each new wave of visiting media, seeking midweek fodder before games.

"I was a walk-on in 1986, my dad's first year as Notre Dame head coach," Skip recounted. "Mostly, I was on special teams, but I did carry the ball once against Purdue [a 41-9 Irish victory], so my career stats here show a net gain of one yard. But in the USC game that year, I got hit with a roughing the punter penalty that helped them take a 37-18 lead. Luckily for me, Notre Dame came back to win 38-37, but Dad still reminds me of that penalty. He says it was his wife's son who committed it."

Roughing the Ref

The competitive fire that never stopped burning in the belly of the Notre Dame coach seldom got out of control because Holtz knew the eyes of fans everywhere were fixed on

Skip Holtz, an Irish assistant coach from 1991-93, made many friends with his low-key style.

him. He didn't mind showing his emotions, although it usually was triggered by a player's failure to execute properly.

They learned from him that little mistakes add up to big consequences, an education that proved as valuable to many of them as the one they got in the classroom.

Holtz went out of his way to make a point to the officials in the final minutes of a 45-20 Irish romp against Brigham Young in 1993. Frustrated by a series of borderline calls against his team, Holtz put a brief hammerlock on referee Tom Thamert to demonstrate what he interpreted as continual holding by BYU.

"There was nothing to it," said Thamert, a veteran Big East Conference referee. "Coach Holtz was excited and he told me, 'My boy's [it was Pete Bercich] being choked.' Then he put his arm around my shoulder, without using any force, and said, 'This is what the BYU player did.'"

Dan Wooldridge, Big East supervisor of officials, added, "The media made it look worse than it was."

Lou Gets the Moosage

Edward "Moose" Krause was one of the most beloved figures to operate under the Golden Dome, from the day in 1930 when Knute Rockne recruited him to play football for the Irish until his death in 1992.

On the Notre Dame campus, it was harder to find a Moose detractor than an atheist, with good reason. One of the most hospitable human beings in sports, the jovial, strapping Krause made instant friends wherever he went.

Krause strode up to a visiting reporter, puffing his ever-present cigar, stuck out his hand, and two strangers began talking like old pals. That was Moose Krause, a man who didn't waste time preaching, because he was too busy practicing the

Longtime Notre Dame athletic director Ed "Moose" Krause (right), a Notre Dame legend, greets actor Pat O'Brien, who played the title role in Knute Rockne, All-American.

ideals of sportsmanship, brotherhood and just plain enjoyment of life.

Moose's stories of Notre Dame lore and legend transmitted the mystique from the Rockne era to thousands of Irish students and fans, who passed them along to their kids and grandkids. "Mr. Notre Dame" was a vital link in that tradition, as well as a legend in his own right. It was easy for Lou Holtz, a man with a sense of history and an appreciation for stories about the feats of Notre Dame's heroes and heroines, to be part of the audience for Moose's tales of Rock, The Gipper and so on. While the slender coach's own legend was growing to rival that of the towering Krause, the two men became good friends.

"Some coaches are born winners, and I've been around long enough to spot one when I see him," Krause said. "Lou Holtz is one of the chosen few."

Still, their mutual admiration society included lots of good-natured ribbing back and forth. At a luncheon packed with fans the day before a home game, Holtz recalled a recent conversation with Krause, who was seated at a nearby table.

"Moose, I really appreciate the nice things you've been telling people about me," Holtz deadpanned. "You said I had a sense of humor, just like Knute Rockne. You said I had a strong work ethic, just like Frank Leahy, and a gift for organization, just like Ara Parseghian."

Without missing a beat, Holtz brought down the house by delivering the punchline.

"You also said I've been losing a lot of games, just like Joe Kuharich."

The Holtz Mystique

When Lou Holtz went on a personal recruiting visit during his Notre Dame coaching days, it immediately turned into an event.

He had—and still has—the kind of personal magnetism that stops traffic and draws crowds wherever he goes. That was proven time and again when the Irish coach went to a high school or a similar setting in pursuit of a blue-chip recruit. The mere fact that Holtz arrived in person enhanced the player's stock, intensifying competition from other big-time colleges to snatch him away.

Wade Wilson, a high school principal, saw the mob scene surrounding those excursions, a level of excitement seldom matched by the arrival of other collegiate visitors.

"No matter what, Lou stayed around until he did what he came to do," Wilson said.

But it remained for Vinny Cerrato, Notre Dame's highly effective recruiting coordinator in 1988-90, to sum up the Lou Effect.

"I say hello to a recruit, Coach Holtz takes over, and I say goodbye," Cerrato shrugged.

The Truth Hurts

Lou Holtz never said, "I doubt we'll make a first down all season." One of his illustrious Notre Dame coaching predecessors, Frank Leahy, did. Leahy's lament came on the eve of an unbeaten campaign for the Irish and still another of the four national championships they racked up under his demanding tutelage.

Those who played for Leahy in that era of dominance can't forget his anguished offerings when they goofed up at practice: "John Lattner! John Lattner! Don't you want Our Lady's school to win?"

Holtz, just as much a stickler for details, could deliver a pointed message as well, when game preparations failed to satisfy his demand for flawless execution. Still, a recurring media perception was that Holtz poor-mouthed his players, while declaring their opponents were unstoppable objects on offense and immovable forces on defense.

"I don't believe I understated the case for Notre Dame and built up every team we played into a bunch of Supermen," Holtz said. "My job was to motivate my players to their full potential. Notre Dame always plays a killer schedule, and beating us is a top priority for everybody we face."

So when *Sports Illustrated* gave one of Holtz's teams an unexpectedly high preseason rating, he couldn't resist the temptation to lob a sardonic response.

"I see [*SI*] listed us in their top 20," Holtz said. "They could get more credibility by using a picture of me in their swimsuit issue."

He's Not Kidding

Gene Corrigan, then Notre Dame's athletic director, hired Lou Holtz away from Minnesota to start rebuilding Irish football fortunes in 1986. Lou's reputation for sprinkling his conversation with jokes preceded him to South Bend, prompting an alumnus to call Corrigan and offer, "We need a coach, not a comedian."

After predicting—correctly, as the record clearly demonstrates—that the Holtz tenure would prove to be no laughing matter, Corrigan told the unhappy fan, "Just look up Knute Rockne's array of one-liners."

It's Serious Business

Holtz had a knack for pinpointing his team's shortcomings with acerbic wit. After Irish special teams didn't perform up to expectations in a scrimmage, Holtz issued a tongue-in-cheek threat to make the players and his assistant coaches vote on whether or not to punt on fourth downs in the upcoming game.

"If things don't get better fast, and somebody asks my advice, I'll tell him, 'Vote no,'" he said.

In reality, as those closest to the often-inscrutable coach suspected, such utterances, as well as classic Holtz malapropisms, were psychological ploys to pinpoint problems in a way that would ease tension and still get his point across.

Lou's Way to WIN

One word—WIN—was the wellspring for 100 Notre Dame victories under Holtz. It stood for "What's Important

Now," his way of erasing distractions to focus on the task at hand.

"If you want to quit, do it tonight," Holtz told the Notre Dame squad before the opening 1988 workout. "It takes about six seconds from the snap to the end of the play. For those six seconds, you have to sacrifice yourself for the team."

The 1988 Irish were willing to make that commitment. They were rewarded with a national championship in only the third season of the Holtz era. Notre Dame came agonizingly close to a couple more before he stepped down in 1996. Along the way, Holtz sent these messages to Irish players:

"Notre Dame should never lose a football game."

"I'd rather have a slow guy going in the right direction than a fast guy going in the wrong direction."

"Your value to this team depends on how far from the football you are."

What Makes Lou Tick?

Lou Holtz found that not even a list of more than 100 challenging lifetime tasks, such as jumping out of an airplane (with a parachute, of course) or becoming Notre Dame's head football coach could keep recharging the level of total commitment he demanded daily of himself.

"You have to have a dream," Holtz said. "When you stop dreaming and just try to preserve what you have, you become the hunted, no longer the hunter. I never got tired of coaching, but maintaining began to wear me down. I don't want to protect the status quo. When you stop trying to get better, the enthusiasm and the energy begin to drain away from whatever the task might be."

Doing the Right Thing

Lou Holtz brushed aside all the speculation and kept it simple when he stepped down as Notre Dame's head coach in 1996, after 11 eventful years.

"It's the right thing to do," he said.

Many diehard Irish fans found that hard to believe. They still display a fierce loyalty to the man and the coach, assuring him a permanent place in the Notre Dame tradition. Holtz overcame a lot of obstacles during his tenure, including serious neck surgery in 1995 to remove a disc compressing his spinal cord. He left behind an eloquent blueprint for success to all those who played for him and others who will don the Blue and Gold for many years to come. A few of Holtz's core beliefs:

"I have only three rules for Notre Dame players: Do what's right. Do your best. Treat others the way you want to be treated."

"There's no substitute for experience, especially with young players. Freshmen don't understand what Notre Dame really means until they become juniors and seniors."

"What I want my teams to do above all else is to perform up to their capabilities. I've always preferred points instead of promises. No player's mouth should write a check his ability can't cash."

Climbing Rock's Mountain

It would have been easy for Holtz to stick around one more season for the half-dozen victories he needed to surpass Knute Rockne's record of 105 and become Notre Dame's all-time winningest coach. This complex man chose not to do so, instead making the emotional decision to resign on November 19, 1996. Right to the end, Holtz told the truth as he saw it.

"It won't be easy for Notre Dame to find a coach with all the intangibles I brought to this job," he said.

As usual, Lou was right.

CHAPTER 7

A Lou's Who
of Irish Talent

Lou Holtz was far from the whole show during his eventful, suspenseful 11 years as Notre Dame's head coach. Like a magnet, Holtz's powerful personality drew a fascinating cast of characters onto center stage under the Golden Dome.

The things they did and the games they won in that span, from 1986 through 1996, are the stuff of Irish legend. Perhaps the most noteworthy aspect of the Holtz regime was the way a blend of coaching ability, burning desire, Notre Dame mystique and an impressive array of terrific athletes produced such a succession of championship runs. Irish fans who rode that emotional roller-coaster share Holtz's conviction that the Irish certainly deserved another title, possibly two more No. 1 berths than the one they won in 1988. They finished second to bitter rival Miami in 1989 and second again in 1993 to Florida State.

"If Notre Dame loses one game, that's the end for us," Holtz noted after the final 1993 polls somehow listed his team at No. 2. The Irish matched Florida State's 11-1 record and beat the Seminoles 31-24 in a memorable Notre Dame Stadium showdown in mid-November, but the poll voters said that wasn't good enough.

Nobody could make that claim about the Holtz-era players. He inherited a strong nucleus from departing Gerry Faust, including 1987 Heisman Trophy winner Tim Brown, and packed the Irish roster with a series of top-notch recruiting classes. Along with athletic ability, these youngsters had class and charisma. It was an extraordinary time for Notre Dame football.

But those players waged a series of battles to gladden the hearts of Fighting Irishmen anywhere Notre Dame fans gathered. The Irish even went to the Emerald Isle in 1996 to win over all—or at least over Navy, 54-27—in Dublin. Except for the rabid minority that demanded an unbroken string of 12-0 finishes, Irish backers who remained in touch with reality realized they were living witnesses to an entertaining, exciting stretch of extremely competitive college football.

The players who struggled to reach the standard of perfect execution set by Holtz never quite got there, but they tried, and succeeded, often enough to win 100 games under him. Along the way, they had a wild and wonderful ride, frequently turning his demanding game preparation into valuable life lessons. Win or lose on the scoreboard, the Holtz lineups were studded with winners.

Powlus Powers Up—and Down

In many ways, the major symbol of Lou Holtz's ups and downs at Notre Dame was the sturdy, battle-scarred body of quarterback Ron Powlus. He came to South Bend in 1993 with the sort of fanfare usually reserved for emperors or rock stars. ESPN analyst Beano Cook predicted Powlus would win not one but two Heisman Trophies while leading the Irish to new heights. Powlus was helpless to protect himself against such hyperbole, so he wore that mission impossible around his neck like an albatross for the next five years.

Ron Powlus, a prolific passer, fought through tough luck for much of his Notre Dame career.

"What I went through at Notre Dame taught me there's no situation I can't handle," Powlus said as he finished his tenure in an Irish uniform. "I had some big games and we had winning teams, but it fell short of all those superlatives people expected of us. I walked away knowing I'll never quit, no matter how bad things get."

The main thing Powlus couldn't protect himself from was injuries. Holtz was on the verge of naming the freshman phenom his starting quarterback for 1993, a surprising move from a coach who equated experience with the error-free performance he prized above all else. Almost as soon as Holtz spoke, the luck of the Irish turned bad for him and Powlus. On a late play of the final preseason scrimmage, the freshman quarterback's collarbone got snapped on a pile-driving tackle by hulking veteran linemen Bryant Young, Jim Flanigan and Oliver Gibson. Just like that, Powlus was out for the year and senior journeyman Kevin McDougal became the starting quarterback.

Ironically, the Irish almost made Cook's prediction of renewed glory come true in 1993, except that Powlus was watching from the sidelines. His delayed debut turned out to be a brilliant show against Northwestern in the 1994 opener at Chicago's Soldier Field, including completing 18 of 24 passes, four for touchdowns.

When Powlus's arrival at the postgame media room was delayed, Holtz had an explanation.

"Ron's out walking on Lake Michigan," he said.

But the expected miracles didn't take place often enough to satisfy Irish fans. A broken left arm in his junior season was proof that Powlus often had to run for his life behind porous pass protection. Still, Powlus showed class and poise, refusing to lash out at the evaluations of outsiders.

"My injury gave Kevin McDougal his chance to play as a senior, and he made good," Powlus pointed out. "I had my time at Notre Dame and I can live with that."

New Sheriff in Town

When Lou Holtz strode into the room for his first meeting with the Notre Dame team he had just inherited from Gerry

Faust, the players didn't know what to expect. It took only a minute for them to find out.

Tired, humiliated and depressed when the 1985 season and the Faust regime both ended with a painful 58-7 beating at Miami, the players survived a stormy trip back to campus, slept briefly and slumped in their chairs, awaiting the new coach. Holtz entered, promptly leveling a stony stare at center Chuck Lanza, who was in the front row of the Joyce Center auditorium.

"If you want to play football for me, you better sit up straight and pay attention," Holtz told him. His words, and especially his tone, went through the room like an electric current. No translator was needed.

This little guy with glasses, stooped shoulders and a lisp meant business.

Lanza straightened up and the Irish straightened out. By the time Lanza graduated in 1987, the Irish were on the doorstep of a national championship and he was a true believer in the iron-fisted Holtz method.

"Coach Holtz is tough, but he knows how to get a team ready for every game," Lanza said. "He makes us work hard, and we do it, because he works harder. This man gets inside your head and pushes you to do things the way he wants them done."

The Mark of Zorich

Chris Zorich was almost as effective at easing the tension on the sidelines as he was as anchoring a ferocious Irish defense on the field. While Notre Dame geared up for the customary man-killing 1990 schedule, the undersized (a modest 266 pounds), overachieving nose tackle summed up the situation with a quip that even made the coaching staff chuckle.

"As I see it, our biggest problem this season will be keeping Coach Holtz calm on the sidelines," Zorich deadpanned.

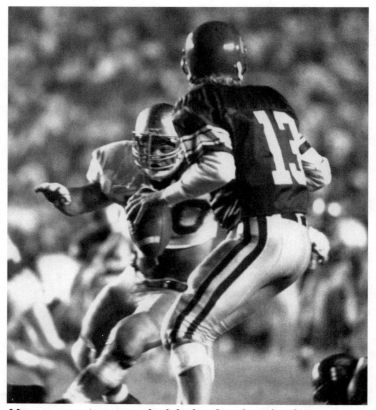

Many an opposing quarterback had to face the sight of Notre Dame's defensive firebrand, Chris Zorich, charging at him.

The Real Spirit of Notre Dame

Chris Zorich is a walking, talking commercial for the ideals that great universities are supposed to teach, treasure and embody. With this gentle giant, it goes way beyond football. Zorich practices what many merely preach.

Once he put on a helmet and pads at Notre Dame and later with the Chicago Bears, "Zorro" underwent a personality change, from Dr. Jekyll to Mr. Hyde. Even at practice, his relentless effort awed teammates, boosted temperatures past the boiling point and caused coaches to cringe in fear of unplanned skirmishes. That kind of intensity, a predictable product of Zorich's boyhood fight to survive on Chicago's tough South Side, made him into an All-America football player.

Much more importantly, the lessons he learned from his mother, Zora, helped him to become an outstanding man. She gave him the confidence to outlast homesickness and the classroom grind and he capped his career by winning the 1990 Lombardi Award as the nation's top college lineman.

"Nobody did more to make things turn out right for me," Zorich said. "I still stutter, but I don't look at my shoes any more when I'm talking to people. I get letters from kids seven and eight years old, asking how they can make it like I did."

Zorich responds to those pleas through his own Chicago-based foundation and a hands-on approach that gives youngsters options to escape poverty, gangs and drugs, reaching out for a better life. Like Warrick Dunn of the Atlanta Falcons, this real-life hero now does things far more important than his football feats.

It's in loving memory of his mother, who died soon after Chris returned from the 1991 Orange Bowl, and also in gratitude for his success story as an Irish student-athlete.

"Notre Dame changes people, and it changed me more than I ever thought possible," Zorich said.

"When I hurt my knee [against Pittsburgh in 1990], I started worrying about my career and feeling sorry for myself. Then I remembered visiting cancer patients at the Texas Children's Hospital. Those kids lost their hair from radiation treatments, but they laughed and played games with me.

"Even if I never had made it to the NFL, coming to Notre Dame would be worth everything I went through to get there."

An Easy Choice

Lou Holtz and his recruiting staff didn't have to work very hard to land Lyron Cobbins, who turned into a dependable line-backer from 1993-96. The youngster from Kansas City, Kansas, also was sought by Miami, UCLA and USC, among other schools, but he felt a lot safer at Notre Dame.

"When I visited Notre Dame, all Bryant Young and Anthony Peterson talked to me about was what I wanted to do with my life. They treated me with respect, and it really touched me. When John Robinson [USC coach] called to ask why I didn't visit there, I just told him, 'I'm going to Notre Dame.'"

Lou's No Linguist

Bob Chmiel, recruiting coordinator and assistant coach for Lou Holtz, found it doubly easy to communicate with Irish tight end Pete Chryplewicz, because both of them spoke Polish. That led to an incident in the 1996 Orange Bowl that Chmiel still enjoys recounting on his WSBT sports talk radio show in South Bend.

Thomas Krug took over for injured Ron Powlus in that game against Florida State. Chryplewicz did an outstanding job of protecting him until he misread a signal, giving blitzing Seminoles a clear shot at the quarterback. While the dazed Krug was recuperating, Holtz ordered the tight end to the sidelines, the usual penalty for a missed assignment.

"Pete stood there, cursing in Polish, while Krug tried to get the next play called," Chmiel said. "But Lou kept looking at Pete, asking, 'What's he saying?' I told Holtz Pete was blaming himself for the hit on Krug. Instead of watching the 25-second clock run down or sending in the play, Lou just stood there, shaking his head. Finally, he told me, 'Isn't that something, being able to communicate in another language?'

"We lost the game [31-26], so it didn't seem very funny at the time. But every time I think about Lou Holtz going off into his own little world, right in the middle of a game, I have to laugh."

The Tradition Lives

Losing drove Ryan Leahy wild when the 290-pound offensive guard became the third generation of his family to play for Notre Dame. He's living proof that heredity matters. His grandfather, Frank Leahy, played for Knute Rockne (1928-29) and later coached the Irish to four of their 11 national championships.

And his father, Jim, played in 1968 for coach Ara Parseghian.

"I can't stand to lose," Ryan said. "It makes me do crazy things."

That sort of fire in the belly came as a surprise to coach Lou Holtz when the younger Leahy played for him in 1992-95.

"At first, Ryan Leahy seemed like the most unemotional player I ever coached," Holtz said. "He sure didn't sound like Frank Leahy, so I figured he must have been adopted."

Rocketing to Fame

Raghib "Rocket" Ismail was even faster, if that's possible, off the football field. At the mere sight of a camera, a microphone or a poised pencil hovering over a reporter's notebook, the Rocket Man could approach the speed of light, streaking in the other direction.

There was his memorable postgame escape from quote-hungry media on October 20, 1990, after the Irish knocked off

No. 2 Miami, 29-20. An adoring throng waited outside the Notre Dame Stadium gates for a glimpse of their hero. Ismail's 94-yard touchdown runback of a kickoff capped a brilliant show by the 175-pound thunderbolt, blowing away the Hurricanes with his 268 all-purpose yards. It was a satisfying payback for the Irish and their fans in the final game of a desperately fought intersectional series that had seen Miami win five of the previous six meetings. The losers admitted Rocket was too elusive for them, but they should have stuck around to witness his getaway after the final whistle.

"I didn't want to spend three hours signing autographs, because my mom was at the game," Ismail explained. "Spending time with her is more important than answering a bunch of [media] questions."

How did he manage the vanishing act? Ismail simply folded his slender frame into a cart, hidden by a pile of dirty laundry, to get wheeled past the crowd by the crew of student managers and whisked out of sight.

Rocket was just as invisible or, more accurately, uncatchable when enemy tacklers took aim at him for three blazing years (1988-90) in an Irish jersey. The pinnacle was his pair of touchdown kickoff returns before a stunned Michigan Stadium mob in 1989 ("I was kind of surprised when they kicked the ball to me the second time," Ismail said), although the Wolverines couldn't say they hadn't been warned. He did the same thing to Rice a year earlier.

Ironically, perhaps the most amazing runback of this phenomenal athlete's college career was the one that didn't count in the 1991 Orange Bowl. Bob Logan got a bird's-eye view and still lists that moment as one of the most electrifying in his half-century of sportswriting. With Notre Dame trailing 10-9, Ismail grabbed a Colorado punt and streaked untouched down the right sideline, 91 yards to the apparent winning score.

Transfixed, Logan stood on that sideline, watching the Rocket roar straight toward him. An anguished moan arose from Colorado fans seated behind the end zone, only to be

Raghib "Rocket" Ismail breaks free against Miami for one of his many crowd-pleasing kick returns.

erased a second later by gleeful bellows at the sight of a flag far upfield. Irish safety Greg Davis got called for a borderline clip, although Ismail already was in the clear and the contact appeared incidental, making the Buffaloes' victory and national championship even more frustrating for Notre Dame fans.

"I barely got my head in front of the guy [Colorado's Tim James], but when the ref threw the flag, I knew it was on me," the downcast Davis said.

(Don't) Fight, Team, Fight

Miami's rough-and-ready Hurricanes invaded Notre Dame Stadium in 1988, for what turned out to be the real national championship game. A pregame incident, precipitated when the 'Canes left the field running through the home team's warmup drill, only heightened the atmosphere.

Officially, decorum required coach Lou Holtz to frown on such temper tantrums, so he issued a perfunctory "Tut, tut" for the nationwide TV audience. Unofficially, he told the Irish, "If they want to go again after the game, I'll be right with you. But leave Jimmy Johnson for me." Fortunately, Notre Dame's 31-30 triumph in an all-time thriller put the coach and his players in the mood to party, not punch.

Not so when it happened again the following year. This time the guest villains were USC's Trojans, and their pregame pileup with Notre Dame players in the tunnel leading to the field was a no-holds-barred dandy.

It might have been worse if the enraged Holtz hadn't plowed into the pile of bodies, personally pulling them apart.

"I was so mad I wanted to whip the world, and that's dangerous for a 150-pound man," Holtz said. "I promise it will never happen again."

Even after Notre Dame came from behind to edge the Trojans 28-24, Holtz was in anything but a celebratory mood. He read the riot act to his team, delivering a threat that shocked Irish players and fans alike.

"This should have been avoided by Notre Dame, no matter who was at fault," Holtz snapped. "If anything like this recurs, I will not coach another game. Mark it down."

Linebacker Ned Bolcar, a co-captain and team leader, said the players didn't take the Holtz bombshell seriously at first.

"We figured here's a guy who loves coaching too much to give it up," Bolcar noted. "But then, when Lou told the media the same thing he told us, we knew he wasn't kidding."

Lou Gets Through

Ricky Watters got the kind of coaching from Lou Holtz that eventually turned the headstrong tailback into an NFL standout. The master psychologist knew how to light a fire under Watters after a sluggish start by the junior in 1989. When Watters went disco dancing to celebrate a 41-27 victory over Air Force, Holtz did a verbal tap dance on him.

"Notre Dame tailbacks are supposed to take so much punishment, they spend Sunday in bed instead of dancing," Holtz said. "We need people willing to sacrifice their bodies to play that position."

The coach also called Watters into his office to remind him that NFL scouts wrote attitude, as well as talent, into their reports. Ricky got the message and responded.

"Coach Holtz told me I was not having the kind of year I'm capable of," Watters said. "That made me turn up the intensity a notch and start playing my heart out."

Mirer Makes His Mark

Rick Mirer would have been a fitting subject for *Hoosiers II*, or some such film treatment. The same feel-good elements that made *Rudy* such a hit were there for Rick, with a few major differences. Unlike Rudy Ruettiger, who got on and off the field for 27 seconds of fame before a cheering Notre Dame Stadium crowd in 1975, Mirer ran the Irish offense for the better parts of three seasons (1990-92).

This tough, level-headed youngster racked up impressive stats. He was a local product, from nearby Goshen, Indiana, and the Irish won 29 games with him at the controls. Like all Notre Dame quarterbacks, Mirer learned to accept life in a fishbowl under the Golden Dome.

"It's neat to get an encouraging phone call from Joe Montana during the week, but once we're in the huddle, it's time to forget the rah-rah stuff," the no-nonsense Mirer said when he won the starting job. "I can't rely on advice from Montana or worry about what the fans think of me."

Maybe Mirer's lack of flash and dash made fans underrate him. Without the charisma of Chris Zorich or the game-breaking potential of Rocket Ismail, this meat-and-potatoes dropback passer would have had to lead Notre Dame to a national championship to get his just due. As it was, the Irish climbed lots of mountains with him, never quite reaching he summit. Still, Mirer occasionally provided a magic moment to match the one in 1990, when his pass bounced off the pads of Michigan State defender Todd Murray, into the arms of Irish receiver Adrian Jarrell to spark the game-winning touchdown drive in East Lansing.

"I'm not saying divine intervention helps us win football games like this," said Lou Holtz, who frequently hinted at such things. "It's just that Notre Dame is a special place."

Taylor Made

Offensive linemen labor in obscurity; even the best of them fail to receive recognition for the battles they wage in the trenches up front, where football games are won or lost. Aaron Taylor was the rare exception to that rule. The 6'4", 280-pound block of granite from Concord, California, was a four-year Notre Dame stud, virtually impossible to beat one on one. Taylor switched from guard back to tackle as a senior and was named the Irish captain in 1993, opening the door for an explosive attack that took them to the brink of the national championship.

"When we needed to find running room, the backs learned to follow number 75, clearing a path for us," said fullback Ray Zellars, who filled the big shoes of departed Jerome Bettis on the 11-1 Notre Dame powerhouse of 1993.

Taylor, a first-round NFL draft pick, earned the championship ring that eluded him in 1993, protecting quarterback Brett Favre when the Green Bay Packers won the 1997 Super Bowl.

Lucky 13 for Rossum

It took just 13 seconds for Allen Rossum to follow instructions to the letter, setting the stage for Notre Dame's 1996 romp over Purdue. Rossum took the opening kickoff where coach Lou Holtz told him to, straight up the middle for a 99-yard touchdown runback. The Irish sauntered from there to a 35-0 whitewash, giving Holtz a perfect 11-0 slate against Purdue in nose-to-nose confrontations with his intrastate rival. Not all of them were that easy, and none were that well-predicted.

"We call that runback Middle Match," Rossum said, replaying the textbook execution in his head. "In our Friday night relaxation time, Coach Holtz told me what was going to happen on our first kickoff return. He said, 'You'll take the ball up the middle and go all the way.' I thought I was dreaming when his prophecy came true. I saw the hole open 10 feet wide, got a block from Ronnie Nicks and headed for the end zone."

"Never had that happen before," insisted Holtz, although he'd certainly tried often enough. "We went over the opening kickoff verbatim. The ball goes to Rossum, everybody gets his block and he scores. That's just the way it worked out."

The Real Deal

Jamie Spencer had his ups and down as an Irish fullback from 1995-98. By the time he was a senior, Spencer began to understand how the collegiate experience had prepared him to cope with real life.

"After four years at Notre Dame, I realize what it takes to get through," Spencer summed it up. "Athletic skill is not enough, unless it's combined with more important factors. I've learned to balance physical ability with mental discipline.

"Competition goes way beyond the football field, to our social and academic encounters. What I've been through here enables me to interact with people, even if I don't agree with them."

The Irish Rumbling Back

"I got finesse, but I don't use it much," Jerome Bettis said.

Why should he? That would be like asking an M-1 tank to tiptoe through the tulips. With a full head of steam, Bettis looked like a cross between Earl Campbell and Bronko Nagurski, two of the all-time blockbuster running backs. A deceptively quick, 245-pound bundle of raw power, he put the fullback spot smack in the middle of Notre Dame's offensive mix by rushing for 972 yards and scoring 20 touchdowns as a sophomore in 1991.

"Jerome Bettis can be as good as Jerome Bettis wants to be," gushed new Irish running backs coach Earle Mosely, arriving the following season to watch the pile-driving fullback flatten would-be tacklers in spring drills.

Bettis didn't disagree with that assessment, and neither did coach Lou Holtz. From an erratic freshman, Bettis blossomed almost overnight into a potential superstar.

"I punish [opponents] when I need to," Bettis described his slam-bang running style. "When Walter Payton got pursued to the sidelines, he never tried to run out of bounds. That's the way I want to play."

After Bettis pulverized Florida in the 1992 Sugar Bowl, carrying the Irish to a 39-28 upset of its third-ranked opponent with his three-TD rampage, there seemed no stopping him. The Irish finished 10-1-1 and No. 4 in the final polls, and a season later Bettis went to the NFL a year early.

"The great players are the ones you hear coaches telling each other, 'Did you see what he did today in practice?'" Holtz sighed when Bettis departed. "We were starting to talk that way about Jerome."

No Kick Coming

Football kickers are either heroes or bums. Yet there's no shortage of strong-legged youngsters, anxious to stick their head—or in this case, their foot —into the lion's mouth of those do-or-die situations. Even hearing about the agony and ecstasy Jim Sanson endured at Notre Dame doesn't seem to discourage them.

Sanson's sometimes erratic boots on the practice field in 1996 earned the freshman the title of "Foul Ball" from coach Lou Holtz. That was the way Holtz tested his players, probing to find out if they could reach down for the last ounce of nerve and skill in the clutch. Sanson could, and did. His 39-yard bulls-eye, with no time left, beat Texas, 27-24, at Darrell Royal Stadium in Austin in 1996, adding a new chapter to the book of dramatic Irish comebacks.

"I told [Holtz], 'I'm going to keep proving you wrong every week,'" Sanson said, savoring his moment of triumph.

It was the peak of a career that had a few valleys. Sanson hit bottom at the end of 1996 by missing an extra point at USC that enabled the Trojans to tie, then win 27-20 win in overtime in Holtz's final game at Notre Dame. It cost Notre Dame a potential lucrative bowl bid, but Sanson handled the adversity better than a few fans who heaped abuse on him. He got the last laugh on them in 1999, when the senior recovered a fumbled USC kickoff to seal a 25-24 Irish comeback in Notre Dame Stadium.

"That erased all the frustration," Sanson said. "The good and the bad are over now. A kicker learns to have a short memory."

Culver's Spirit Survives

Rodney Culver put others ahead of himself, and Notre Dame's football team ahead of his own ego. During the national championship season of 1988, the talented tailback switched positions to fullback, easing an injury shortage in the offensive backfield. Then, when highly touted freshman Jerome Bettis made an immediate impact in 1990, Culver turned the fullback chores over to him and returned to his old position.

"That was the example Rodney Culver showed this football team," Lou Holtz said of the man who became the Irish captain in 1991. "His blend of leadership and performance was a stabilizing influence, especially on the younger players."

Culver was a role model in his hometown, Detroit, as well. He bridged social, racial and other barriers with strength of mind and spirit, plus an outgoing nature. As an NFL back at Indianapolis and San Diego, the message he delivered to youths was that their lives were not limited to a choice between flipping burgers or pushing drugs. Active in the Big Brothers program, he was a powerful example to kids that making the effort to get an education was the right way to go. When Culver and his wife, Karen, died in a 1996 plane crash, the news sent shock-

Rodney Culver eludes an Air Force tackler to pick up yardage. Culver wrote a bright chapter in Notre Dame's book of legends.

waves through Notre Dame and wherever former teammates gathered.

"Rodney was Notre Dame football," said tailback Reggie Brooks. "He had a mature wisdom, and we just naturally wanted to follow him."

CHAPTER 8

Play Like a Champion This Season

Lou Lights the Fire

From the moment he walked onto the campus to grab hold of Notre Dame's football fortunes, Lou Holtz began planning what happened in 1988—the perfect season. Ara Parseghian, aware from bitter experience what a rare blend of total dedication, maximum effort, superb skill and a little bit of luck it took, was one who believed Holtz could pull it off. Holtz was another, although he cannily played the underdog card whenever signs of overconfidence cropped up on that overachieving '88 squad.

Asked when fall camp opened if the Irish could get through their brutal schedule unbeaten, Holtz had a ready rejoinder:

"Most people don't expect us to get through our first two games unbeaten."

True enough, especially since the list of departing seniors was headed by Tim Brown, the 1987 Heisman Trophy winner. Besides, the long trek to the Fiesta Bowl began with two Big Ten booby traps, Michigan in Notre Dame Stadium and at Michigan State.

Boo-Hoo by Bo

The Irish were ready for Michigan when that annual eye-gouging derby resumed. A good thing, because crusty coach Bo Schembechler had been inciting the Wolverines by rerunning film of the previous season's 26-7 humiliation by the Irish. On his part, Holtz got ready for more than just a victory over Michigan by moving Frank Stams from fullback to defensive end. Stams's mental and physical toughness lit the fuse that never went out.

"We knew defense would have to carry us until Tony Rice and Rocket Ismail got their timing down," Stams said. "Right after we lost the Cotton Bowl [35-10 to Texas A&M on January 1, 1988], Coach Holtz called the team together and told us what we had to do to win the national championship. We worked all that spring and summer to get ready, and then we went out and did it."

That oration must have ranked right up there with Knute Rockne's "Win one for the Gipper" classic.

The Irish won not one but 23 straight games after that, a streak that led to the doorstep—although not to the throne room—of a second straight No. 1 finish.

Ho, Ho, Ho (Ho)

But a lot of that might not have happened unless the Irish put first things first. Their first obstacle was Michigan, on September 10, 1988, a battle fully worthy of this drama-packed series. With Rice misfiring on his first nine passes, Notre Dame

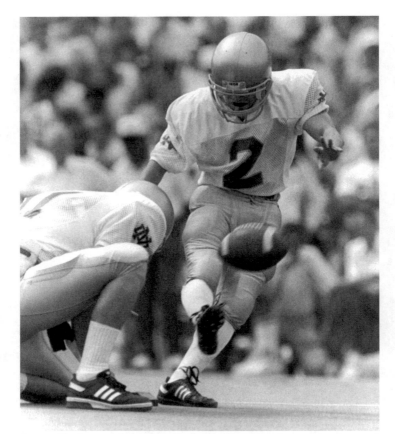

Reggie Ho boots a field goal for the Irish. His tireless work ethic paid off with a 4-for-4 performance in the nail-biting 1988 victory over Michigan.

had to put the foot back in football to escape with a 19-17 thriller. It was supplied by the tenacious toe of five-foot-five placekicker Reggie Ho. He booted four field goals, the last a 26-yarder with just over a minute left to provide the winning points.

"The privilege of being at Notre Dame is all I want," said the 135-pound Ho, a walk-on from Kaneohe, Hawaii, who declined to ask for a scholarship, even after those four field goals made him the coast-to-coast toast of Irish fandom. "I didn't think about missing [the last one], with everybody depending on me."

Ho didn't, but the Irish almost missed out on his clutch performance, because the little guy lacked the strong leg to boom 'em through the uprights from 40 to 50 yards out. Still, he practiced fanatically, digging holes in snow-covered Cartier Field over the winter, so his holder could place the ball down.

In a typical motivation tactic, Holtz spurred the untested kicker on with a tongue-in-cheek remark.

"We have a lot of confidence in Reggie, especially from five yards in," the Irish coach said.

In the end, Ho's determination to keep at it earned him the chance to boot the Wolverines at the end.

"Reggie's out there kicking every day," the Irish coach noted approvingly "He's obviously not Garo Yepremian. What he does is work to get better."

It Takes the Breaks

Even without scoring an offensive touchdown, Notre Dame outplayed a tough team in that 1988 opener. Michigan refused to quit, coming tantalizingly close to pulling it out when Mike Gillette's 48-yard try on the game's last play hooked wide right. By that slender margin, the season-long chain of success began turning into tempered steel for the Irish.

Years later, veterans on that team recalled how they realized the razor-thin difference between success and failure, even while the young players joined Irish fans stampeding from the stands in a jubilant celebration.

"Michigan was a game we had to win," agreed tailback Mark Green, a co-captain and spark plug for the eventual champs. "If that last field goal [by Gillette] had been a little straighter, a lot of our dreams would have gone down the drain.

We were so fired up by Coach Holtz, and you could see the confidence grow every time we walked off a winner. Early in the season, guys like Frank Stams, Wes Pritchett, Boo Williams and I were whooping it up in the locker room, trying to reassure the kids. Before the Miami game, they were doing the same thing for us."

Rice-ing to the Occasion

Tony Rice seldom piled up impressive statistics during his two and a half years (1987-89) as Notre Dame's starting quarterback. All he did was win. The easy-riding youngster overcame his share of obstacles to rack up a remarkable 28-3 record in games with him under center for the Irish. A rare blend of

An unheralded quarterback, Tony Rice proved his major talent was winning.

quickness, poise and leadership enabled the quiet Rice to make lots of noise on offense. He had a knack for making things happen at crunch time, just as he found ways to succeed in Notre Dame's demanding academic arena. Before Rice played a down, he had to deal with media reports that he'd been admitted despite subpar test scores. That added to the pressure on an African-American quarterback at a time when outdated stereotypes still lingered.

Because Rice believed in himself, he soon made believers of the skeptics. The carpers and fault-finders had a hard time explaining away Rice's success as a student and a football player. He overcame mechanical flaws at quarterback, notably a tendency to throw wobbly, inaccurate passes, with the same work ethic that mastered his classwork, leading to a degree in psychology.

"Notre Dame was the right school for me," Rice said after spearheading the Irish to a 24-1 slate in his final two seasons. "It's a place where people care about each other. The history and tradition are alive. I got criticized for coming here, but I was willing to make the effort, whatever it took, to make good."

Game of the Century?

Notre Dame vs. Miami in 1988 can stake a legitimate claim to that status. The buildup began early, while both teams survived hurdles to remain unscathed and climb toward the summit of the weekly Top 25 polls. When game week finally arrived in mid-October, pandemonium accompanied it to South Bend.

For once, the X-and-O analysts were overshadowed by the intensely human drama unfolding in the shadow of Notre Dame Stadium. The Hurricanes stormed into town, confidently prepared to extend their 36-game victory streak in the regular season by winning on the road for the 21st straight time. Their attitude had been fueled by four straight wipeouts of Notre Dame, with a 133-20 combined victory margin adding to the humiliation. Besides the No. 1 ranking, the defending national champs brought along passing wizard Steve Walsh, brash coach Jimmy Johnson and their trademark confidence.

They believed that would be more than enough to overcome the Notre Dame mystique and the fourth-ranked, underdog Irish. As things turned out in a classic that lived up to its blockbuster ballyhoo, the 'Canes came agonizingly close to being right. Almost, but not quite. Anyway, it was a wild, wonderful week, capped by the rare spectacle of the event actually surpassing the hype. For coach Lou Holtz and his players, the struggle to get to this point proved worth the pain.

The Flash Point

Darrell "Flash" Gordon was there when Lou Holtz arrived, and Gordon worked his way into a starting spot at defensive end. He saw Holtz hone a talented group of individuals to the edge of greatness as a team. Gordon still laughs at the books and magazine articles that tried to portray Holtz as so obsessed with winning that he condoned almost anything to whip them into shape.

"The coach had all kinds of ways to motivate us," Gordon said. "What he wanted to do was bring us together. Every player had to find his own way to reach his potential. If he didn't make that effort, somebody willing to pay the price would take his place in the lineup. I remember Coach Holtz telling jokes and doing tricks at practice, trying to ease the pressure when exams were coming up. He did his share of yelling and I saw him grab a few helmets when guys made the same mistakes over again, but we knew why it happened."

The Bruise Brothers

Another pair of battle-tested Irish seniors, defensive end Frank Stams and linebacker Wes Pritchett, set an example in the locker room and on the field. With all-out effort in practice, as well as games, they helped mine the potential of such budding stars as Chris Zorich and Rocket Ismail. Equally important was their ability to keep everybody loose with pranks and patter, while pumping up some who needed a shot in the arm or a kick in the butt.

"Wes and I kind of played the role, doing what we thought was needed," Stams recalled. "But there was so much chemistry on that team, we could have fun and skip the speeches. Lou Holtz always kept one step ahead of the players, giving us another mountain to climb every week."

Ever-Ready Ned

Ned Bolcar had a knack for providing what was needed, on and off the football field. That's why he was an All-American linebacker, a mainstay for Notre Dame's unbeaten 1988 national championship team and a role model for younger teammates. With all that, he still found time to serve as a locker room prankster with fellow free spirit Frank Stams.

"It bothers me when high-profile athletes treat people badly," Bolcar said. "If fans want to talk to me or ask for an autograph, I try to spend a little time with them. Sometimes it's difficult, because they can get too excited, but I don't think I'm more important than they are. I try to explain that there's lots more to my life than just football."

Catholics 31, Convicts 30

"Catholics vs. Convicts" was just one of many unauthorized T-shirt slogans on the chests of Irish fans when their team tackled Miami on October 15, 1988. It was a showdown to remember, probably pivoting on one crucial call in the fourth quarter. Just about to score the tying touchdown for the Hurricanes, Cleveland Gary instead coughed up the ball when safety George Streeter slammed into him and linebacker Michael Stonebreaker recovered at Notre Dame's one-yard line. Still, this 31-30 Irish triumph wasn't over till the final frantic play, when Miami's two-point conversion victory bid bit the dust in the end zone, along with the 'Canes' national championship hopes.

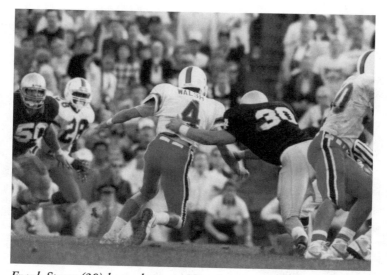

Frank Stams (30) bears down on Miami quarterback Steve Walsh (4) in the classic "Catholics vs. Convicts" battle.

Irish Stand Pat

Irish eyes were smiling and Irish spirits soaring when safety Pat Terrell leaped to frustrate Steve Walsh's pass in the left corner of the south end zone at Notre Dame Stadium. Terrell's heroics prevented Miami from stunning the Irish, 32-31, in the final second of a magnificent college football game. The entire season, as well as a slice of Fighting Irish football history, hung and swung in the balance at that instant. For the home fans, it turned out right, touching off a gigantic emotional outburst on the field.

Notre Dame rode that narrow escape to an unblemished season and the 1988 national championship. A dozen years later, that moment and game were rated tops of the 1900s in Notre Dame's "Century of Greatness" web site balloting. Terrell and defensive end Frank Stams were the co-heroes for a defense that forced seven turnovers by the high-powered Hurricanes. It was a role Terrell savored.

"Everything is more fun on days like this," he said. "When one play can make the difference, I feel it's up to me to make that play. Some guys won't take risks when it's all on the line, because they're afraid to make mistakes. I don't look at things that way. There's a difference between confidence and cockiness."

Barry Alvarez, Lou Holtz's defensive coordinator, knew Miami made a fatal mistake by throwing to Terrell's side of the field for what would have been the crushing two-point conversion.

"We called a timeout and asked the defense for pressure on Walsh and perfect execution in the secondary," Alvarez said. "That's exactly what we got."

USC Forced to Flee

So it came down to Notre Dame needing a victory over ancient nemesis USC. These rivals hungered for the chance to spoil each other's seasons and both had their turns at doing just that.

The Trojans cost Ara Parseghian a national title in 1964 by coming from behind to pin a 20-17 heartbreaker on the top-ranked Irish.

Now, 24 years later, it was No. 1 Notre Dame facing No. 2 USC on the same Los Angeles Coliseum turf.

Quarterback Rodney Peete's mobility and pinpoint passing, the smart money said, would enable the Trojans to prevail over Tony Rice's erratic arm.

Naturally, Rice fired a 55-yard strike to Rocket Ismail on Notre Dame's first play from scrimmage. With the USC defense bunched to keep the Irish in the hole on their two-yard line, the Rocket simply exploded into the clear. He stumbled, preventing a touchdown on that play, but Notre Dame had all the firepower it needed for an impressive 27-10 romp. The Irish defense rushed Peete off his feet, and the battered quarterback was no factor. Rice definitely was, passing only nine times for 91 yards and rushing for 86 more, 65 of them on an option scamper for the game's first score.

Peete's Retreat

"We read all the Heisman hype about Rodney Peete," said Irish linebacker Wes Pritchett after he helped chase USC quarterback Peete out of the 1988 trophy race, which was won by Oklahoma State's Barry Sanders. "Our challenge was to blitz him out of his rhythm and shut him down."

Lou Horses Around

Obviously feeling his oats after going 3-0 against USC, Lou Holtz tossed a postgame quip at Traveler, the Trojans' equine mascot.

"They have this horse that runs around the field when USC scores," the Irish coach said. "First time I saw that, I thought I was at the race track."

Holtz also denied sending offensive hotshots Ricky Watters and Tony Brooks home on the eve of the USC game was a psychological ploy after the two rookies were late for a Friday evening team meeting. Even if it wasn't, it worked.

Yale Locked Out

Irish receiver Pat Eilers needed no pep talks to prepare for the Fiesta Bowl, which would reward his team or West Virginia, the only other unbeaten major power, with the 1988 national championship. Eilers transferred from Yale to Notre Dame after the 1985 season because he wanted to combine academic excellence with big-time athletic competition. Yale once ranked among college football's elite, but when the Ivy League de-emphasized sports in the 1950s, the era of Eli gridiron glory vanished abruptly.

"At Notre Dame, you can do it all," Eilers said. "Academics and athletics are both important here. If we win, everything Notre Dame stands for gets magnified. I'm amazed by the way people all over the country care about this team."

A Great Way for the Irish

Nobody expected the final step to be that easy. It was, because Notre Dame's offense and defense both clicked on the same day—January 2, 1989. It was the day South Bend had been awaiting for 11 years, since the Irish leaped from No. 5 to the top spot in the final 1977 polls by routing Texas 38-10 in the Cotton Bowl.

When a fierce pass rush pounced on highly touted West Virginia quarterback Major Harris early and often, the Mountaineers became a minor threat. Notre Dame led 16-0 before the outclassed opponent could make a first down. Scoring on four of their first five possessions in Sun Devil Stadium, the Irish turned the Fiesta Bowl into a 34-21 punchout party.

By far the best quarterback on display in the one-sided affair was Tony Rice. Still generally underrated and unappreciated elsewhere in the country, this soft-spoken junior suddenly found himself totally appreciated by once-skeptical Notre Dame fans. It's easy to see why. Against Harris and USC's Rodney Peete in back-to-back matchups, Rice outperformed both of them soundly in the only place where it really counted—on the scoreboard.

An Oscar for Tony

"Everybody put us down, all season," Rice said, handling the postgame media rush with the same quiet efficiency he employed against opposing pass rushers throughout this 12-0 Notre Dame victory march.

"We had something to prove as a team, but I've never tried to prove I'm an outstanding quarterback.

"I didn't come here to show I'm better than Major Harris. Our only goal was a national championship for Notre Dame."

They got it, almost without breaking a sweat, but it's a good thing Rice was not in charge of determining his own classroom grades. After running and passing the Mountaineers dizzy, personally accounting for 288 of the 455 yards racked up by the Irish offense, the modest field general insisted, "I'd give myself a grade of B for today. No way I'd ever get an A."

No. 11 and Counting

When the final polls came out the next morning, the all-night celebration resumed. Notre Dame was No. 1 on both wire service lists, sealing national championship No. 11.

"I was not going to talk about what this team deserved until the results were in," coach Lou Holtz said. "The only poll I read is the last one every season. Now it's time to answer the people who said Notre Dame wasn't good enough to go all the way."

Heck of a Finish

For the 17 Irish seniors, it was an emotional payoff that made up for some hard times. Offensive tackle Andy Heck was a freshman on the 1985 team that ended the season by getting embarrassed, 58-7, in Miami.

"This is a whole new feeling," Heck said. "When Coach Holtz came in [in 1986], we didn't ask him why he wanted things done a certain way. We just did them, and look at us now."

Holtz continued the coaching tradition of winning a national championship in his third year at Notre Dame, just like Frank Leahy, Ara Parseghian and Dan Devine. His secret?

"We turned things around by recruiting football players with speed, not converted track men," Holtz replied. "If you get the toughest guy in the world and he's not where the ball is, what good is he?"

They're Everywhere

No matter where Notre Dame plays, Irish fans show up, even when it's not easy being green. Parkersburg, West Virginia, was not exactly Leprechaun Land in 1988, especially while the West Virginia Mountaineers were bracing to face Notre Dame in a Fiesta Bowl showdown between undefeated teams, with a national title on the line. That didn't deter Kevin Kearney, six, from wearing his Notre Dame hat to school every day.

"Kevin knows all about the Golden Dome," said his mother, a Notre Dame graduate, along with her husband. "Since we moved to West Virginia, we cheer for the Mountaineers, but not in this game. Kevin wouldn't hear of it."

CHAPTER 9

Davie's Irish— Highs and Lows

Faust Fodder

In 1997, I was speaking in Detroit to an industrial group. I was not that far from Notre Dame, and Rudy Sharkey, who coached with me at Akron, was traveling with me. Rudy had never seen Notre Dame. Rudy was coaching at Mt. Union College in Alliance, Ohio, where he helped them to five NCAA Division III national championships.

"Well, we're only two and a half hours from Notre Dame," I said. "Do you want to drive over? They're in spring football and we can watch." Rudy didn't have practice that day, so we decided to do that.

So I called Coach Davie and told him we were on our way over and, if it was okay with him, I'd like to introduce him to Rudy Sharkey and say hello. He said, "Great."

So we got over there before they practiced. We went in and saw Coach Davie and sat and talked with him for a while.

"We have practice," he said. "Would you like to come?"

"I'd love to come," I said.

So we went over to the Loftus Center, where they were starting practice indoors. Coach came over to me and asked if I'd like to speak to the team. I told him I'd love to.

So Coach Davie got the whole football team together. That was the first time that I'd talked to a Notre Dame team since I left in 1985.

I'll never forget this as long as I live. I sort of broke up and tears were coming down my cheeks at the end. It was an emotional time for me, talking to the Notre Dame team.

"You have four, maybe five years at Notre Dame," I told them. "Don't look back at those four or five years without giving your best. Because when you leave, it's over. When it's over, you want to be able to look in the mirror and say that I've given my best for my teammates and for Notre Dame.

"As I look back, I gave my best but I didn't get the job done. You men, you get the job done."

It was a time that I cherish and I thank Coach Davie for giving me the opportunity to speak to his football team.

✛

Bob Davie took Irish fans on a wild ride through his five years as head coach. Sky-high expectations always take the field along with Notre Dame teams, so Davie faced some amount of pressure to build on the Lou Holtz legend. It didn't happen often enough, despite a couple of respectable 9-3 seasons sandwiched in between three years of .500 football.

Irish coach Bob Davie joins the Notre Dame Stadium crowd in saluting an Irish touchdown.

Understandably, Davie's tour of duty, from 1997 through 2001, did not always produce a barrel of laughs—or victories. He compiled a 35-25 record, good enough to hang around lots of places, but numbers that were merely average at Notre Dame.

Things were different when Holtz stepped aside briefly in 1995 to undergo spinal surgery. A neck disc, perhaps weakened by an old football injury, began compressing the coach's spine.

Doctors warned it eventually would either paralyze him or kill him unless he submitted to an operation.

In his second year as Irish defensive coordinator, after Holtz hired him away from Texas A&M, Davie knew only something that serious could take his boss off the sideline. Along with Notre Dame players, fans and the rest of the coaching staff, the new guy in town answered the call.

In truth, the fired-up Irish were so inspired that they probably could have manhandled the Green Bay Packers in Notre Dame Stadium on Saturday, September 16, 1995. That was four days after the successful neck surgery and two weeks before Davie's 41st birthday. Vanderbilt was the designated victim that sunny afternoon, and the Commodores got it in the neck, 41-0. The postgame jubilation in the stands, on the field and in the winners' locker room resembled the final fadeout of *Rudy.*

By the time Holtz, shrugging off the pain, returned to the sidelines for good for the November 4 Navy game, Davie had piled up lots of bonus points with the Irish faithful. His blend of youthful enthusiasm, coaching skills and boyish grin marked him as a front-runner in the head coaching future books. His chance didn't figure to happen at Notre Dame, because nobody expected Holtz to depart the Golden Dome without being carried away feet first.

But Lou stunned the college football world by quitting just before the end of the 1996 season. So there was Davie, ready, willing and able to fill the void. Presiding over his last pep rally, the night before a 62-0 slaughter of Rutgers, Holtz asked the emotional throng of Irish true believers to be patient with their new coach. They were—until Davie lost four straight games after winning his head coaching debut over Georgia Tech, 17-13, in renovated, enlarged Notre Dame Stadium on September 6, 1997.

The honeymoon was semi-sweet, and too short. Fresh-faced and confident, Davie said, "Notre Dame is where any coach would want to be," then plunged into the thankless—not to mention impossible—task of replacing an irreplaceable bastion of Irish football tradition.

Light Touch the Right Touch?

"I'm going to sleep really well," Davie said. That was just before his first media joust as Notre Dame's head coach. "I'm not going to be blind-sided by what's coming."

"It's great to be the undefeated, unscored-on head coach at Notre Dame," Davie assessed that early euphoria.

Caught up in the excitement of the moment, many Irish players saluted the changing of the guard.

"Bob Davie's a terrific coach," said quarterback Ron Powlus, an old-school drop-back passer, obviously hoping the defensive specialist would swing the offensive pendulum away from Notre Dame's traditional grind-it-out option ground game.

"The guys like Coach Davie and they trust him," added fullback Marc Edwards. "He brought a lot of energy to our defense, so I figure he can do that for the whole team.

"This is where I want to be."

Basking in the glow of what looked at first glance like a seamless transition, Davie projected optimism about the job at hand.

"I waited a long time for this job," Davie said. "This is where I want to be for the rest of my career."

He tried to make those rosy forecasts come true by tinkering with the offense to suit the strengths of various quarterbacks, hired well-regarded strength and conditioning coach Mickey Marotti and put renewed emphasis on the performance of Irish special teams.

Ara Adds the Spark

When Ara Parseghian speaks, Notre Dame people listen. So his vote of confidence for Davie carried plenty of weight. Besides that, Ara's genius at shifting players away from the wrong positions and plugging them into the right ones provided plenty of sound advice for the new kid on the block and his aides.

"The key to coaching is knowing how to put all the pieces together," Parseghian pointed out. "I believe Bob can do that. A football team is like a racing car. Take the spark plugs out and it just sits there. But when you tune it up right and get the engine purring, it'll roar around the track."

Davie's Debut

Some Notre Dame fans' misgivings kicked in early when the Irish were knocked off 28-17 at Purdue in the rookie coach's first road venture on September 13, 1997.

"I know I can win here," Davie said. "The first thing I'll try to get rid of at Notre Dame is fear of failure. You can't coach or play if you're worried about screwing something up. I won't worry about the big picture or the magnitude of this job. I won't panic. I don't expect to be judged on every game.

"There's the temptation for any first-time head coach, especially at Notre Dame, to think everything rides on his first season and first recruiting class. Hey, I'm going to be here. I'm totally confident in my ability, so I'll go slowly to make sure I'm doing things the right way. Everybody knows there's a lot of pressure on me. The main thing is to keep it in perspective."

Grumblers Gather Steam

Despite some similarities in the script from Lou Holtz's 5-6 first season in 1986 with the Irish, 1997 was a whole different story for Bob Davie. His Irish couldn't get it all together until past midseason, when they came on with a 5-0 rush, including one of the high points of the Davie era, a 24-6 pounding of 11th-ranked LSU in the lair of the Tigers, one of college football's most inhospitable cages for visitors.

A 23-7 loss at home to Michigan State on September 20, 1997, knocked the 1-2 Irish out of the top 25 polls for the rest of the season.

"Things are unusually quiet out there," the coach said, noting the abrupt absence of enthusiasm among the students. "The coaches can huddle together and isolate themselves, but our players live in the dorms and they have to deal with people. Our team's attitude is remarkable, so we have to tell them the truth. I haven't said we're close to being a winning team. We don't have a Chris Zorich or Aaron Taylor type to keep us fired up. It would help to have somebody step up and take charge on the field."

Denson Rushes to Success

There had to be a reason why a little halfback made so many big gains—enough to become Notre Dame's all-time rushing leader, galloping for 4,318 yards. It was all the more amazing because the speedy youngster was shifted to defensive back in his first Notre Dame fall camp. That ended quickly when the Irish couldn't pick up a crucial first down on third and short, dooming their drive for the winning field goal in a shocking 17-15 upset loss to Northwestern on September 2, 1995. The next day, Denson was back where he belonged, on the offensive side of the ball.

The 5'10" battering ram weighed only 189 pounds as a sophomore, thought by some to be too small to make a major impact, so Denson wasn't expected to better his 5.1 yards per carry average of 1995

"I intend to be the best tailback who ever played for Notre Dame," Denson proclaimed.

Tailback Autry Denson breaks away from a Navy pursuer, en route to becoming Notre Dame's No. 1 all-time ground gainer.

Well, George Gipp was a halfback, but Denson ended up almost doubling the Gipper's 2,341 career rushing yards. In fact, once he starting galloping, this dynamo from Fort Lauderdale, Florida, didn't stop until he had surpassed the 4,131 yards churned out by Allen Pinkett from 1982-85. Denson made that brash prophecy come true, at least statistically, finishing his brilliant four-year run in 1998 as the No. 1 Irish ground-gainer. How did he survive to rack up such numbers against beefier, bigger defenders?

"I'm an instinctive runner, but I learned to change pace and stay low, so tacklers couldn't slam into me," Denson said. "I take the hardest hits around the shoulders and keep driving with my legs."

No Mich.-ed Opportunity

In Davie's second turn at the helm, few knew what to expect in the 1998 season opener. The Irish punched across 30 unanswered points to stun the Michigan Wolverines, the defending national champs, 36-20. Quarterback Jarious Jackson pushed all the right buttons on the new-fangled option attack that tailback Autry Denson gleefully labeled "execution football."

An apt choice of words, because Denson galloped for a career-high 162 yards while the bewildered Wolverines got eliminated by an electrifying six and a half-minute, 17-point Irish power surge in the third quarter.

"I've never seen Notre Dame Stadium lit up the way it was today," Jackson added.

East Lansing Lancing

One of the longer nights in Notre Dame's century-plus of gridiron exploits took place in Spartan Stadium on September 12, 1998. The Irish fell 45-23 to Michigan State. Coming just a week after they had kicked off the season by stunning No. 5 Michigan, 36-20 in Notre Dame Stadium, it was all the harder to swallow. Even so, this ambush was not entirely the fault of Davie or his team.

The Irish walked into an emotional booby trap and got carried out on their shields. Maybe no team in the country could have survived this trap laid by Michigan State and its fans in the overheated setting of that stadium, jam-packed with 74,267 spectators. The Irish were out of it in a hurry when the Spartans scored early and often. A national TV audience gazed either mournfully, gleefully or disbelievingly, depending on their rooting tendencies, at the halftime scoreboard. Notre Dame trailed 42-3 at that point.

Truthfully, all of that night's drama was compacted into a few seconds before the opening kickoff.

Cornerback Amp Campbell, only hours out of the hospital after spinal fusion surgery, walked out with his Michigan State teammates for the coin toss.

"I cried," Spartans tailback Sedrick Irvin confessed. "Whatever it took to earn a game ball for Amp, we did it."

The crowd went wild, and so did the Spartans. From an emotional standpoint, the game was over before it started, although that didn't make the trip back to South Bend any easier.

Jackson in Action

Jarious Jackson lived up to the tradition of such mobile Irish quarterbacks as Tony Rice and Kevin McDougal. Those two competed for national championships, Rice taking Notre Dame to the promised land in 1988 and McDougal just missing in 1993. Jackson never got that close in his century-closing shot at it. The sturdy 228-pounder from Tupelo, Mississippi, had the arm, the legs, the talent and the heart to do it all when he ran the show in 1998-99, but fate rolled snake eyes for him in those tantalizing, frustrating 9-3 and 5-7 seasons.

When he wasn't injured, the gifted quarterback got the job done, despite lugging much of the the burden of the offense on his broad back. He toiled for a different offensive coordinator each of his starting seasons—ex-Purdue coach Jim Colletto in '98; and Kevin Rogers, former ringmaster of Syracuse's aerial circus, in '99. Rogers, who molded Donovan McNabb into the second pick of the 1998 NFL draft, summed up the challenge awaiting Jackson.

"Virtually every play is going to live or die with Jarious," he said.

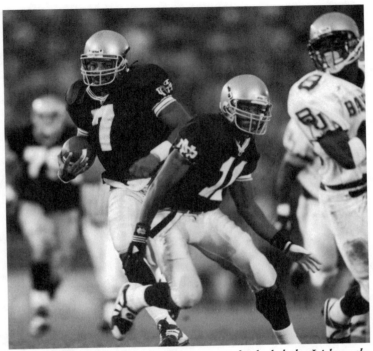

Jarious Jackson, a talented, elusive quarterback, led the Irish to the Gator Bowl in 1998.

That proved prophetic. Notre Dame's ground-pounding, bone-crunching offensive tradition continued to go airborne in Bob Davie's tenure (1997-2001) as head coach. He started with a drop-back pocket passer, Ron Powlus, returning as a fifth-year senior in 1997, then turned to the option, rollout, scrambling style that suited a mobile trio—Jackson, Arnaz Battle and Carlyle Holiday.

Jackson was the best of the bunch, but had to wait until he was a junior to electrify Notre Dame Stadium as a pinpoint passer and elusive runner. Only a knee injury late in 1998 denied Jackson and the Irish a major bowl bid, the chance he deserved to showcase his big-time talent. The fifth-year senior gave an awed Notre Dame Stadium audience something to go wild about on October 2, 1999, recalling memories of legendary Joe Montana by sparking a magnificent comeback to stun Oklahoma, 34-30. Jackson ran through the Sooners for 107 yards and passed them dizzy, completing 15 of 21 for 276 yards and two touchdowns, in a Heisman Trophy-worthy performance.

"I remember Jarious standing there with tears rolling down his face," said Mike Rosenthal one of three 1998 Irish captains, describing the postgame scene after an emotional 39-36 victory over LSU. "It wasn't because he got hurt on the last play, trying to take a safety. He was watching the seniors sing the Victory March, and got caught up in their emotion. That's the kind of team guy Jarious Jackson is."

Quick Shift

Going with the new trend in college quarterbacking, Notre Dame recruiters replaced drop-back signal caller Ron Powlus with the fast pace of such elusive scramblers as Jarious Jackson, Arnaz Battle and Carlyle Holiday. That was supposed to take them into the 21st century on flying feet, with the threat of quick athletes turning option runs into big gains. Keeping a wary eye on that, the theory held, deterred defenses from loading up with the nine-in-the-box formation, favored by Big Ten teams to stuff the running game.

It worked well for Jackson, who sparked the Irish to the doorstep of a big-time bowl bid in 1998, until fate intervened, dealing him a bad break and the Irish a bigger one. With victory over LSU wrapped up on November 21, Jackson sprinted into his own end zone to run out the clock by taking a safety. He did, but a vengeful tackle tore his right knee ligament, tearing the heart out of Notre Dame's jubilation.

"We decided not to risk a blocked punt or giving LSU a chance to run it back," the grim-faced Davie said. "Nobody figured Jarious would get hurt on the play."

What everybody figured as soon as Jackson went down, though, was that winning the season finale at USC might turn into mission impossible. Without Jackson, green-as-grass freshman understudy Battle and junior Eric Chappell had to take the quarterback reins. Notre Dame was doomed to a third straight setback by its traditional foe, this one a 10-0 defeat in Los Angeles Coliseum. Just like the traumatic 27-20 loss in the same place to the same team two years earlier, the defeat cost Notre Dame a lucrative bowl bid.

Irons in the Fire

Grant Irons was one of the finest human beings to play for Notre Dame, where class and character are not exactly unheard of. Unfortunately, a seemingly endless string of injuries prevented him from living up to his potential as one of Notre Dame's best linebackers or defensive ends

His brother, Jarrett, was an All-American at Michigan, but Grant chose Notre Dame. He never regretted it, despite the double-barrelled pain of getting hurt early and often in his college career and having to watch from the sidelines. Irons earned respect for playing at less than full efficiency, especially when the 275-pound Texan needed IV fluids to ward off heat prostration during a steamy 24-10 victory over Texas A&M in 2000.

A broken leg, plus severe shoulder and knee ailments also plagued Irons throughout his career, but couldn't dampen his enthusiasm. He gave equal time to a wide spectrum of worthy campus causes in 1997-2000, departing with an enviable record as both a student and an athlete.

"I see myself as more than Grant Irons, the football player," Irons said.

So does his wide circle of friends.

"Rudy" Boiman?

Rocky Boiman played the way Rudy would have if the celebrated sub only had the same talent to match his desire. Linebacker Boiman's playing career was just as dramatic, but much longer, with his flaming red hair and matching spirit bolstering the Irish defense from 1998 to 2001. He was fun to watch and talk to, because his quotes seemed like they were straight from the script of another favorite film for Notre Dame fans—*Knute Rockne, All-American*.

"Nothing's out of reach for Notre Dame, not even the national championship," Boiman said, shaking off the frustrating 27-24 overtime loss to Nebraska in 2001.

His teammates took him seriously, because Boiman was literally ready to bleed for them. A cleat cut in the Nebraska game severed his wrist artery, with blood spurting out in a crimson spray. To nobody's surprise, Boiman was back at his linebacking post a few plays later.

Battle-Tested

Arnaz Battle was an unsung hero throughout his career at Notre Dame. The classy young man from Shreveport, Louisiana, waited his turn to be the starting quarterback, only to see the injury jinx strike early in 2000, just when he started to emerge as the offensive leader. Instead of brooding or blaming, Battle came back as a receiver, only to get hurt again.

It would have been enough to discourage many players, but Battle had learned how to survive more than physical pain as a youngster. His younger brother, Brandon, died at age three in a swimming pool accident, a family tragedy that enabled Arnaz to keep football and other daily problems in perspective. Battle wears a tattoo depicting the young boy on his left shoulder as a permanent reminder.

"Brandon would have been a better player than me," Battle said. "I got it [the tattoo] to keep him with me wherever I go."

The way Battle did whatever he could to help out, especially the position switch, made him a team leader. Only the sixth Notre Dame player ever to wear five football monograms, he was named one of the 2002 season captains.

Matt's Where It's At

Matt LoVecchio was the calmest man in South Bend while leading Notre Dame on a wild charge through the 2000 season. Just 18 when he made his first collegiate start at quarterback for the Irish, this cool cat from New Jersey promptly proved he was not America's typical teenager. LoVecchio's low-key personality did not produce startling quotes for the media, but he quickly won the respect of veteran players and the adulation of giddy Notre Dame fans.

With starter Arnaz Battle benched by a broken wrist and backup Gary Godsey unable to ignite the offense, freshman LoVecchio inherited the No. 1 quarterback role against Stanford on October 7, 2000. It was the start of a seven-game winning streak that propelled the Irish into a No. 10 national ranking and a Fiesta Bowl matchup with Oregon State.

But getting LoVecchio to boast about such startling statistics as his lone interception in 125 passing attempts proved to be an impossible task. The most quotable quote about this publicity-shy youngster was this colossal understatement from his offensive coordinator, Kevin Rogers, who said, "There's a certain amount of calm to Matt."

Fred Stengel, the coach at Bergen Catholic in Oradell, New Jersey, where LoVecchio was the sparkplug of back-to-back- state prep champs, spelled it out even more clearly: "Matt could work on an algebra problem in a street fight."

LoVecchio did little, at least publicly, to dispel that image. "Taking things in stride is important for me," he said over and over, while the Irish flourished under his confident leadership.

Beneath that placid exterior, though, LoVecchio had a burning desire to excel and to win. But things began to unravel for him and Irish coach Bob Davie in a 41-9 Fiesta Bowl pounding from Oregon State, and LoVecchio transferred to Indiana for the rest of his college career before the 2003 season.

Rose Dream Wilts

New bowl eligibility rules had even led to speculation that the Irish might return to the Rose Bowl for the first time since 1925—if they finished the 1998 season with a 10-1 record. Instead, they wound up 9-3 when the shutout at USC sent Notre Dame off to the Gator Bowl. Jackson came back to see action in that game, but couldn't prevent a 35-28 loss to Georgia Tech, coached by George O'Leary, who was destined to make a brief appearance on the Notre Dame stage a few years later.

Mich.-management

The 1999 schedule started with a 48-13 cakewalk. It came over Kansas, but what happened in the next two weeks was definitely not a stroll on the Yellow Brick Road. The Irish were in position to win at Michigan and again at Purdue, although they ran out of time in both places. The same sort of tough luck that dogged Davie all too often dealt him a double whammy, starting September 4 in Michigan Stadium.

A puzzling "excessive celebration" penalty after an innocuous gesture by Bobby Brown, just after Notre Dame scored the go-ahead touchdown in the fourth quarter, helped jump-start the strange sequence that gave the Wolverines an undeserved gift. So did a borderline late-hit penalty on Irish safety Ron Israel while Michigan chugged to the decisive score. There still was time for a miracle finish, but Notre Dame lost precious seconds when Jarious Jackson got sacked, so the game ended with still another squabble about whether the clock should have stopped for an Irish first down. Painful as it was to watch, the hurt was worse for the players.

Maybe Brown should have dropped that two-point conversion pass instead of waggling his hands at a heckler in the stands. The pass gave Notre Dame a 22-19 lead, but the 15-yard penalty on Brown started Michigan toward a comeback touchdown to salvage this bitter struggle, 26-22.

"I have to be a man and admit I gave the momentum back to Michigan," Brown said. "The coach [Bob Davie] should know I wasn't trying to act like a hot dog."

"I don't blame Bobby Brown," Davie said. "I blame myself. We outplayed them, but mistakes beat us."

Déjà Vu at Purdue

The same frantic finish happened all over again a week later in Ross-Ade Stadium. Unlike the 52-7 and 48-0 demolition derbies inflicted on their traditional intrastate rival during the Lou Holtz years, the Irish have had to wage all-out war in recent years. Purdue's 28-23 triumph in 1999 was all that, producing more gut-wrenching frustration for Notre Dame. Time ran out with quarterback Jarious Jackson swarmed under by a Boilermaker blitz at the Purdue goal line.

Spins and Tailspins

The first Irish squad of the new millennium lost a heartbreaker to Nebraska on September 9, 2000, before a Notre Dame Stadium throng that appeared to be split down the middle between boisterous, red-shirted Cornhusker loyalists and apprehensive home fans.

Davie's players responded with a magnificent effort that fell agonizingly short in a terrific struggle. Nebraska was fortunate to depart with a 27-24 overtime decision for the visitors and something of a moral victory for the aroused, frustrated Irish.

Can't Bother Bob

Davie pointed out repeatedly that Notre Dame's traditionally ferocious schedule, facing intersectional powers from coast to coast, made unbeaten Irish football seasons unlikely, if not impossible. He agreed growing parity in the college ranks produced an ever-increasing weekly array of mild to major upsets.

"My team is not influenced by outside issues," the coach kept saying. "This job teaches you to be resilient and minimize the distractions. Realistically, a shot at the national championship for Notre Dame is a few years down the road."

Givens Gives His All

One of the best all-around football players at Notre Dame in Bob Davie's five-year tenure was David Givens, a versatile receiver. He's now proving it again on Sundays as a pass-catch-ing mainstay for the New England Patriots' budding NFL dynasty.

For the Irish, Givens was all over the place, mostly where the action was. He was a special teams standout, making NFL scouts shudder at the sight of this prime prospect sprinting downfield under kickoffs to hurl his body at waves of beefy blockers.

"David could play quarterback if we needed him to," Davie said. "We'll keep using him in a lot of roles."

With a blend of speed and size at 6'3" and 215 pounds, Givens also lacked the self-absorption that hampered the pro careers of such receivers as USC's Keyshawn Johnson. He put playing football ahead of showboating.

"If I could, I'd be in on every play," Givens said.

The Final Season

Davie knew his fifth season needed a Notre Dame turnaround after a 41-9 loss to Oregon State in the 2001 Fiesta Bowl. His big chance at redemption awaited in Lincoln, Nebraska, where a season-opening rematch with the Cornhuskers demanded intense preparation and 60-minute intensity. But on September 8, the Irish fell behind early, eventually ending in a 27-10 loss to Nebraska.

The Irish split their remaining 10 games for an overall 5-6 mark in 2001, and Davie was let go right after the season-ending 24-18 Irish victory, December 1 at Purdue.

No Alibis

Converted soccer player Shane Walton became the catalyst of a terrific defensive secondary in 2002, making Tyrone

Willingham's coaching debut at Notre Dame a headline-grabbing success. Still, Walton felt badly that Willingham's predecessor, Bob Davie, took the brunt of blame for a 5-6 record in his final season.

"It's a direct reflection on the players," said Walton, who teamed with Vontez Duff to give the Irish perhaps the nation's top cornerback tandem. "Coach Davie can't control a blown assignment. He did his job, but the players have to step up and take responsibility."

A Time for Change

"Any Notre Dame football coach finds something new to worry about every day," Davie said. "But the only thing he should worry about is winning. Ara Parseghian told me that when I took this job. He was right."

So ended the Davie era. Everything else that needed to be said about it already had been hashed and rehashed into bits. Those might-have-beens blew away on South Bend's December wind, smaller than the vanished dreams of Davie being able to make Irish football shake down some new thunder in a new century. Without bitterness or rancor, Davie bowed to the inevitable.

"Looks like I won't get to swim in my new pool," the ex-coach said of the house he'd just built for his family.

CHAPTER 10

Ty's Not Playing for a Tie

Faust Fodder

For the Pittsburgh game at Notre Dame on October 12, 2002, I flew up with a bunch of friends of mine on their plane. Notre Dame was 5-0 at the time, and there was a sense of excitement throughout the campus. I was taking my friends around, showing them the campus. I took them over and showed them the football facilities over in the Joyce Center.

I was going into the southwest entrance and walked by the parking area. My old parking spot was the first space, and I saw a sport utility vehicle there. I saw this family having a tailgate there. I assumed right away since that was my parking space when I was there that that was Ty Willingham's space.

I went up to the people and kiddingly said, "You know, you're parking in my old parking space here." They all started to laugh.

"I'm Gerry Faust," I said to the woman who appeared to be the mother, who later introduced herself as Kim Willingham, Tyrone's wife.

"Coach," she said, "It's great to meet you."

"Are you the Willingham family?" I asked. And she said they were.

"I'm glad that you have my old parking space," I said. "And I just want to wish you the very best and tell Coach I haven't met him yet, but he's started out great. I'm proud and happy for him. Tell him to keep it going and tell him I said hello."

"Well, it was a pleasure to meet you coach and thank you so much," Kim Willingham said.

I went back and showed my friends the offices and took them upstairs where the memorabilia was on the second floor. I pointed out where my name was up there with the Monogram winners.

We left and went to Mike Leep's tailgate party, then went over to the stadium and went up in the press box and watched the game. Notre Dame won, 14-6, to move to 6-0 on the year.

A day later, Coach Willingham left me a voicemail telling me he was glad that I met his family and he really appreciated my comments.

When I got the voicemail, I called back and I talked to him for about 20 minutes. I told him I didn't want to bother him, because I knew how busy he was. But I told him that I was really happy for him and happy for Notre Dame, the way things were going.

We had a great talk. We laughed about a lot of things. I was really impressed with him. Since then, we've met. I've been with him two or three times and I've enjoyed it every time. I just think he's a class act and I'm praying and rooting for him to get the program back on track, which I really feel he'll do. He represents Notre Dame the way it should be represented.

One thing Coach Willingham has done is make his players aware of the great history of Notre Dame football. Former stars like Joe Theismann and Joe Montana have returned to address the team and the school's place in the history of the game is stressed to players and recruits.

I think it's so important that Notre Dame football should never lose sight—and the players should always be reminded—of the past. The past is what made Notre Dame what it's all about. I always tried to keep it up. Coaches have always done that. It's important that students know the past because the past is what made the present and the future.

When a young man understands the tradition of Notre Dame football—the great players, the great coaches, the student body and the subway alumni—they play harder because they know what it stands for. I don't think there's a school in the country that can match Notre Dame's heritage. A lot of schools have a rich tradition, but it doesn't compare to Notre Dame.

✢

Ty Spells It Out

Tyrone Willingham clearly enjoys a challenge. As the man responsible for balancing the storied Irish tradition with the realities of the new college football roadmap, his is a delicate balancing act.

When it comes down to defining his mission at Notre Dame, the coach spells out the big picture with unmistakable clarity. While the Irish were struggling to get back on the victory trail near the end of a frustrating 2003 season, Willingham was asked about his perception of the football program at this unique university.

"The Notre Dame tradition was built on excellence," he replied. "It consists of winning football games, developing quality young people and responding to every situation with integrity. My expectation for this program is to win the next football game we play."

After seven years as Stanford's head coach, Willingham knew he was stepping into an entirely different world when he left Palo Alto to deal with a red-hot South Bend situation. He provided a thought-provoking definition of an atmospheric gap far wider than the 2,000 miles separating Northern California from Northern Indiana.

"It's more at Notre Dame," Willingham said, leaving little doubt about the real meaning of the word "more"—expectations, pressure, fervor and everything else.   "Whether you're winning or going through difficult times, it's just more."

Winning Window

When Willingham won his first eight games at the Irish helm in 2002, euphoria erupted at warp speed, bringing thousands, if not millions, of fans back into the fold. Notre Dame's resurgence was one of the sporting world's hottest topics that season, with wait-and-see skepticism dwindling week by week as the unbeaten run lengthened. Finally, when the Irish upset Florida State, 34-24, on the Seminoles' own turf in Tallahassee to peak at No. 4 in the polls, the frenzy rivaled the aftermath of their 31-24 triumph over the top-ranked Seminoles in 1993.

Naturally, Willingham got the lion's share of credit for catapulting his team back into the national spotlight. The coach managed that media blitz in his customary even-keel manner, trying not to let the fans' overconfidence affect the players. Willingham kept the focus on football, as he did by surfing diplomatically through the tidal wave of publicity when he left Stanford to become the first black head coach of any Notre Dame sport.

He had fought through many obstacles to earn the post of gatekeeper for Notre Dame's football tradition, tackling that challenge with the inner strength that had marked his climb through the coaching ranks. Few expected such success in his Irish debut, and if Willingham himself did, he wasn't inclined to let on.

The Coaching Art

Willingham employs several motivational tools to sharpen that little extra edge for the Irish. They range from the powerful force of his personality to coaching techniques to subtle ways of seeking a psychological advantage over the upcoming week's foe. He has the knack of pushing the right button for individual players.

Sending the "Go Irish" message to crowds of supporters at pep rallies, pregame luncheons and similar affairs is a chore Willingham performs masterfully. The ability to articulate his mission for Notre Dame's football program quickly became a valuable asset. Willingham has proven as effective with his calm, poised approach as Lou Holtz was while pulling out all the stops of emotional oratory. Equally effective is the way Willingham unleashes his droll sense of humor.

A Straight Shooter

Willingham's approach to coaching—and to life in general—is not hard to figure out. He is a traditionalist, with deeply rooted convictions about core values. For instance, standards in many areas of American society keep getting lowered to the vanishing point. Willingham, in sharp contrast, sets a lofty performance goal for himself and for his players. What it boils down to is "Accept nothing less than the best you're capable of doing in any situation."

That's why this coach and this university proved compatible. Notre Dame's national identity was built on football victories, but the school has gained worldwide respect based on academic excellence and outstanding performance, both in the classroom and on the playing field.

Willingham gained respect in many circles while at Stanford, and lists national security advisor (and Notre Dame alumna) Condoleezza Rice as a close friend. What Tyrone Willingham believes in is what Notre Dame believes in. When he says, "I respect the tradition of this place," he's talking about a lot more than Knute Rockne and the Four Horsemen.

Here's Where It's At

How does a coach create the mental edge that makes the difference between a good team and a great team?

Willingham: "What a coach has to bring to any program is stability. Once everybody knows their roles in the system and starts to have some success, confidence grows. When players learn that consistency is the key, they can settle down and provide the same level of performance on every play. There will be setbacks and disappointments. It's up to the coaches to make it clear that the best players will play, especially those who are ready to keep doing their assigned tasks the same way, improving with repetition. Familiarity with a system makes it easier to adapt when your opponent comes up with new wrinkles. The emotion has to come from within, but players need a plan flexible enough to meet changing situations. Above all, no matter who we're playing, our coaching staff stresses that we'll do whatever it takes to win."

What part does your sense of humor play in that process?

Willingham: "Coaching is teaching. Humor is just one of many motivational tools. It's easier to get a point across with a light touch now and then. Practice is hard, intense work, so if we can find something to smile about, it eases the tension and helps the team to prepare for the task at hand. I'm not a big-picture coach. I want my assistants and players to feel what they have to do is focus on our next game, instead of dwelling on the past or jumping ahead."

Frank Leahy, Ara Parseghian and Lou Holtz all spent more than 10 years trying to cope with the constant pressure every Notre Dame coach feels. What about you?

Willingham: "If I last 10 years at Notre Dame, I'll have a great career."

Irish Choice Is Clear

Willingham'a credentials stood out so sharply they might as well have been etched in the night sky over the Golden Dome. His interest in the Notre Dame job was evident, so all Irish athletic director Kevin White needed in December, 2001 was permission from his Stanford counterpart, Ted Leland, to talk with their head coach.

"What Ty did best was mold our young people," Leland said. "He's a role model and an outstanding educator. I told Kevin, 'Don't talk with Ty again unless you're offering him the job.'"

So on New Year's Day, 2002, Willingham and his family met the media in South Bend, opening a new era in Notre Dame football. Why did Stanford let him go without a fight? Leland summed it up three words: "It's Notre Dame."

New Irish coach Tyrone Willingham and wife Kim attend Willingham's introductory press conference with their children (left to right): son Nathaniel and daughters Cassidy and Kelsey.

The Man and the Mission

Notre Dame's president, Rev. Edward A. Malloy, C.S.C., promptly made it clear that Willingham had been hired to be a winning football coach, not to serve as a symbol.

"It has the potential to be described entirely as a social statement," Father Malloy observed of the media fanfare surrounding the news that Irish football fortunes would be determined by an African-American coach. "[Willingham] was chosen because he was the best coach who was appropriate for Notre Dame and all it represents."

White also got straight to the heart of the matter.

"We share a rock-solid belief that Notre Dame can play national championship-caliber football without sacrificing our high academic standards or the integrity of this program," the athletic director said. "[Willingham] understands that challenge better than anyone in his chosen profession."

The new coach was aware the media would contrast his low-key approach with the relentless scrutiny that surrounds every aspect of Notre Dame football.

"This is the most high-profile university in the country," Willingham agreed. "I have always said that if you're doing the right thing, it doesn't matter how bright the lights are. If you're doing the wrong thing, it only takes a flashlight."

The Off-Field Games

Willingham's soft-spoken approach is unfailingly polite, but his meaning is unmistakable. He does not go into exhaustive detail when responding to questions. The coach sets a tone of diplomatic inquiry about such detours. Willingham's technique is to lighten the mood with a quizzical smile and a quip. Instead of dwelling on Xs and Os, he often takes a whimsical detour.

"I'd love it if we had one play in our system," he said when asked while welcoming the media to 2003 preseason practice whether his offense would include a pass to the tight end. "If we had perfect execution of that play and our opponent could not stop it, I'd be very happy."

Moments later, Willingham put preseason predictions in perspective when he was told the crystal ball gazers had pinned a "not that good" label on Notre Dame.

"Not knowing what great reporter wrote that story, it's difficult for me to respond," he said. "If we can win our next game and the last game of the season, we'll be in good shape."

Things didn't work out that way. The Irish nipped Washington State in their overtime opener, but a loss at Syracuse closed the door on a 5-7 campaign.

"It doesn't matter to Coach Willingham who plays," Irish quarterback Brady Quinn said. "We're only interested in putting the best player at each spot. Everyone plays a role. The team has to do the job on the field, but our fans have a role in the stands, too. If they make enough noise, opponents find it hard to run their plays or even think. They can give us the extra boost of confidence players get when they know people are with them, win or lose."

Now That's Balance

When things weren't going well early in 2003, Willingham lost neither his sense of direction nor his sense of humor.

One-sided offensive numbers contributed to road losses at Purdue (23-10) and at Boston College (27-25) in 2003. The Irish rushed for a mere 49 yards against the Boilermakers while picking up 297 through the air. Same outcome at Boston College—47 yards rushing, 350 passing in that setback. In stark contrast, the Irish pulled off a 20-14 upset at Pittsburgh with a whopping 352 rushing yards—262 alone from Julius Jones—and just 33 passing.

Before power-packed USC came to Notre Dame Stadium on October 11, Willingham reflected on the telltale stats from the visits to Purdue and Pittsburgh.

"Against USC, I'm praying for our Purdue passing game and our Pittsburgh running game," he said.

One Line at a Time

When Willingham fields a multiple choice question, he tends to chop it into manageable bits. For instance:

Q: Looking at it from a different perspective, you've played two games. That means four halves. You're down 3-1 in terms of each half. Is Notre Dame football in trouble? Can Notre Dame win a first half and can you put over 38 points on the board?

Willingham: "Interesting perspective. Yes, yes, no, yes, haven't yet."

Q: (About the season-ending injury to linebacker Mike Goolsby) How does this year shape up?

Willingham: "Still shaping."

Q: (About the leg injury that ended placekicker Nick Setta's Irish career) What is Nick's injury exactly?

Willingham: "He's out."

Q: (A reporter's statement) Ara Parseghian once told me he gets mail criticizing the team even when he wins.

Willingham: "In this environment, that's safe to say."

Q: Do fans send you plays to use in the next game?

Willingham: "Never after Tuesday (when the game plan goes in)."

BCS a Real Mess

Ty Willingham couldn't figure out why the Irish loss to Syracuse might have cost USC a berth in the 2003 national championship game. Snubbed by the BCS computers, the Trojans—ranked No. 1 in both the AP and coaches' polls—faced Michigan in the Rose Bowl instead of Oklahoma in the BCS Championship Sugar Bowl. While it's hard for Irish fans, coaches or players to sympathize with archrival USC, most agree that the IRS tax code can be easier to decipher than the BCS.

"My physical education degree doesn't qualify me to understand how it works," Willingham confessed.

The Real Game Plan

"What I want first and foremost for our program is to win," Willingham says. "That never changes. We want to win every game, especially the next game. I've found the best way to do that is to be driven toward what you want. I know what my goals are and I try to keep our team clearly pointed at them. If we can maintain that focus, we can find a way to win."

Subway Alumni Fly, Too

Ty Willingham is constantly reminded of Notre Dame's ferocious fan loyalty. While flying once to South Bend, he met an individual who goes to extraordinary lengths to be there for the Fighting Irish.

"This wasn't a young man," Willingham said. "He told me he flies in from Kansas City every home game weekend to be an usher in Notre Dame Stadium. I don't know how much of the game he gets to see, but people like him are part of the Notre Dame tradition. Wherever I go, they come up and remind me that the Irish are supposed to go 12-0—not just this year or next year, but every year. That's why there's no place like this university."

Heaven Help Us

When Tyrone Willingham dropped this suggestion into the conversation, it took a few seconds for some writers to realize the new Irish coach was just kidding.

"Maybe we'll try cutting some top rows out of the stadium to get a clear view of Touchdown Jesus," he said of the famed 132-foot mosaic on the library wall, with arms upraised. "It would help us to have opponents see that."

All in the Family

As soon as he could, newcomer Ty Willingham played golf with Irish coaching legend Ara Parseghian. It wasn't just a social event or a courtesy call. Willingham got plenty of useful tips from the man who twice led the Irish to national championships, in 1966 and 1973. The main one?

"I told Tyrone to hang up those Ws," Parseghian said. "At Notre Dame, you have to win and keep winning."

Willingham also consulted with Lou Holtz, mastermind of the unbeaten 1988 Irish national champs.

CHAPTER 11

Willing Hands Help Willingham

Forget the Blame Game

No one understands the expectations faced by a Notre Dame coach better than Ara Parseghian, remembering what happened after he masterminded the Irish to a 9-1 record in his 1964 debut.

"We lost two games and tied one in 1965, and some people wrote I wasn't all that good a coach," Parseghian said. "It's unbelievable. But when you win, especially at Notre Dame, they expect it to happen all the time. There will be ups and downs for Ty Willingham. I can see he's doing all the little things right to bring this program back where it belongs."

Willingham appreciated the vote of confidence. He's going about it the way Parseghian did—with excruciating attention to detail. He welcomes advice from former coaches besides Ara, talking things over from time to time with Lou Holtz and Gerry Faust.

A No-Panic Zone

Willingham never had a panic button before he took over at Notre Dame, so the coach felt no need to grope for one at the first sign of misfortune on the field and disillusionment in the stands. He preached the doctrine of better execution through repetition, while repeating that sticking to the plan was the right way to go. With a blend of more experience in his system and freshmen recruited to fit into that system, Willingham is convinced that the Irish again will be national contenders again. How soon?

"Yesterday, if it's up to me," Willingham responded, flashing his deadpan style. "I'm sure you [media] guys expect it to happen tomorrow. All I can tell you is that I want it to happen now. We're not working on any five-year plans here. Notre Dame should be in the hunt [for the national championship] every year, and I believe it will be."

Dream Weaver

Anthony Weaver did not get the All-America recognition he probably deserved at Notre Dame. Maybe it was hopscotching along the defensive front, from tackle to linebacker to end, that cost him. Or perhaps the yo-yo seasons—9-3, 5-7, 9-3, 5-6—the Irish chalked up in his four productive years (1998-2001) as a starter. His brand of humor, infectious spirit and willingness to reach out to younger players made the versatile 286-pounder a tower of strength.

"Wish I could have played one season for Coach [Ty] Willingham," Weaver said after the Baltimore Ravens drafted him. "He made a point of encouraging me when I worked out for NFL scouts, even though I was through at Notre Dame."

Irish Give No Quarter

One of the most memorable plays of Tyrone Willingham's first season at Notre Dame was a pass from a reserve quarterback to a converted quarterback. It was the game-winning play against Michigan State, Willingham's alma mater, that the coach predicted would happen, earning him the nickname of "The Prophet" from his team.

"Last year, I wouldn't believe this could happen," said Pat Dillingham, Notre Dame's walk-on quarterback. "But with what happened after Coach Willingham took over, I saw anything was possible."

That included the impossible dream of Dillingham hitting former quarterback Arnaz Battle with a 60-yard touchdown pass to beat Michigan State, 21-17, on September 21, 2002. It stunned a Spartan Stadium crowd with just over a minute left and starting Irish quarterback Carlyle Holiday on the sideline resting a separated shoulder.

"Right now, I'm feeling no pain," Holiday beamed, greeting ecstatic Notre Dame rooters outside the dressing room.

Baering Down on Defense

Notre Dame defensive coordinator Kent Baer might have almost as much impact on Tyrone Willingham's success at Notre Dame as Willingham himself. Unlike several other top-tier college programs, the Irish do not schedule less challenging opponents early in the season to tune up for tougher foes.

"It looked at times like we weren't playing hard enough on every snap," Baer said of the way his defensive unit learned its lessons in 2003 losses to Michigan, USC and Florida State. "But we're not dealing in excuses around here. Playing a lot of zone on pass defense calls for timing and execution. That comes from experience. Our guys paid for their mistakes earlier in the season, but they stuck with the system. You could see them start-ing to keep the ball in front of them [on pass plays], so we're not getting beat deep much anymore.

"With Justin Tuck giving us a strong pass rush, we can concentrate on improving our efficiency against the run."

Tuck returned to help put the 3-1 closing spurt of 2003 together for the Irish. Graduating linebacker Courtney Watson figures to be performing somewhere in the NFL, because he was consistently around the ball throughout his career. He'll be missed by Baer's unit, along with departing cornerback Vontez Duff, although both 2003 seniors left behind some big-play highlight films to assure their membership in the ranks of all-time Irish standouts.

"To me, Courtney and Vontez personify Notre Dame football," Baer said. "I'd been to Notre Dame Stadium before, when Stanford came here to play, but you can't really under-stand what it means to so many people until you've been around guys like them."

No Faine, No Gain

Jeff Faine, Notre Dame's All-American center, connected with Ty Willingham almost as soon as they met. The rugged senior's admiration for the new Irish coach sent a clear signal to younger teammates, who had total respect for leader of the Irish offensive line. That had much to do with the 8-0 start to Willingham's 2002 debut, rocketing Notre Dame back into the national spotlight.

"Coach Willingham instills confidence in us by the way he attacks every situation and every game," Faine said. "He's not cocky or arrogant. What he does is give us the feeling we can win, no matter what."

Faine became the heart of the Irish offense, literally and physically, by vowing, "Nothing's going to keep me off the field." He proved it, playing in pain through a string of injuries.

A Special Player

Glenn Earl was the kind of player Ty Willingham was looking for when the new coach left Stanford to take the Notre Dame reins in 2002. Fortunately, Willingham didn't have to look very far. Earl, who blocked a potential game-winning field goal against Air Force in 2000, was there, anxious to prove he could be even more than a special teams standout.

He got his chance when the Willingham era opened, starting at safety for an Irish secondary unit that ranked among the nation's best. Injuries kept Earl on the sidelines for most of the 2003 season, but his reputation as a hard hitter made the youngster from Naperville, Illinois, a promising NFL prospect.

"When I got here, they told us special teams would win games for Notre Dame," Earl said. "But for me, it's even more fun at free safety. When our linebackers take on the blockers and the ball carrier gets hung up in traffic, that's my chance to make a tackle they can hear up in the stands."

The Future Is Now

Willingham was fortunate to find two impact players on offense, emerging just when he needed them most. The combination of senior tailback Julius Jones and freshman quarterback Brady Quinn enabled the coach to pull the 2003 season back from the brink of its 2-6 start. Willingham insisted that things were inching in the right direction—and Jones and Quinn aided impressively in that push.

J.J. and B.Q. Take Charge

Before their first and only season together in the Irish backfield ended, Julius Jones and Brady Quinn turned into a one-two offensive punch that made some veteran Notre Dame Stadium gazers pinch themselves. When they were clicking in tandem, the J.J-B.Q. dynamic duo sounded faint echoes of long-ago heroics by the likes of Bertelli-Miller, Lujack-Sitko, Hornung-Morse, Hanratty-Bleier, Montana-Ferguson, and Powlus-Denson.

The unassuming Quinn laid no claim to comparisons with Johnny Lujack or Joe Montana when he took over at quarterback early in a rugged 2003 schedule. If he's injury-free over the next three seasons, though, this 6'4" youngster from Dublin, Ohio has exhibited the potential to become one of college football's premier quarterbacks, while rewriting Notre Dame passing records.

Quarterback Brady Quinn's remarkable poise under pressure as a freshman in 2003 stamped him as the leader of the Irish offense.

"I like what Brady has done for us," Willingham said. "We had to trade limited experience [Carlyle Holiday] for almost no experience at quarterback. Under those conditions, Quinn has been fantastic, and he'll keep getting better."

ABC Sports analyst Bob Griese put the Irish outlook in perspective after Quinn had a tough day, behind an offensive line riddled with injuries, in the season-ending 38-12 loss at Syracuse, a downbeat finish to an upbeat debut for the poised freshman quarterback.

"Quinn is going to be a great quarterback," Griese predicted. "When he gets time to find his receivers, he'll get the ball to them. But no quarterback, especially a freshman, can win without an offensive line that can block for him."

The Brady Bunch

Brady Quinn heard lots of noise from Irish fans while he stood on the Notre Dame Stadium sidelines for the first time as the backup to incumbent starter Carlyle Holiday. That was just the wakeup call for the newcomer in a rapid-fire sequence that saw him wear many hats—sudden starter, savior, and more. At 19, going on 30, the kid from Ohio is stockpiling all of that progress, preparing to use it on Notre Dame's opponents for the next few years.

By the time he's no longer a teenager (he'll turn 20 on October 27, 2004, just four days after Boston College pays a visit to Notre Dame Stadium), Quinn wants to be in full command of Willingham's modified West Coast offense. He agrees with the coach that it should produce a better run-pass ratio, especially through the air.

Honey of a Prospect

Before every game, Brady Quinn gulps down a spoonful of honey. It provides a quick burst of energy, although the easy-going youngster agrees that victory provides a taste that's even sweeter. The honey is just a habit that goes back to his grade-school days.

Quinn's poise under fire impressed his teammates when he stepped in to replace Carlyle Holiday under center early in the 2003 season. He took a lot of punishment, but emerged with valuable experience as the undisputed leader of the Irish offensive unit.

"Brady's a level-headed guy," said Irish receiver Chinedum Ndukwe, a high-school teammate of Quinn's. "He knows the fans will measure him by how many games Notre Dame wins with him at quarterback. That matters to him a lot more than how many passes he completes."

Quinn has the credentials to join the long list of outstanding Irish signal callers, along with boyish good looks and star quality. He enjoys visiting hospitals to talk with ailing children.

"It's easy for football players to overlook how lucky they are," Quinn said. "I don't want to forget about young people who never get that chance."

Fresh Pressure for Frosh

What made Willingham and his assistants agree that a true freshman should get thrown into the fray any Notre Dame starting quarterback must face? It wasn't purely a hope-and-pray decision, because Quinn had been demonstrating that he wasn't America's typical teenager since the day he showed up for fall practice. Neither cocky nor brash, he carried himself with a balance of poise and confidence that quickly caught the coaches' eyes.

But Holiday had earned the starting nod in 2002, helping to make Willingham the toast of the Golden Dome with an 8-0 start and a 10-3 finish. When the Irish offense struggled early in 2003, the door was open for a new Irish quarterback, and Quinn quickly took over.

"Brady's driven to be the best and help this team win," Willingham noted. "He's very eager to be our starting quarterback."

Hail of a Farewell

Lou Holtz said it at least 10 times a season during his 11 years Notre Dame.

"I really believe Our Lady up there on the Golden Dome looks out for us," Lou would say when things went right for the Irish. Or even if he wanted to reach back for extra inspiration—especially when his team faced favored opponents—from a higher authority.

In the case of Julius Jones, maybe Holtz was right. If Jones had stuck it out at Notre Dame, he would have played his final season in 2002. Instead, he left school for a year, but the Irish came up with a 1,000-yard rusher (actually, 1,085 yards) in Ryan Grant, so Ty Willingham's upbeat coaching debut in 2002 took place without him.

But when some spark was needed in 2003, a human hurricane arose to blow away would-be tacklers and waft a fresh breeze of hope. That one-man offense turned out to be none other than Julius Jones, recycled, rededicated and relentless. For Jones, the last act was a hit show of record-breaking proportions.

200 Times Three

The boost Jones provided for Notre Dame's offense went far beyond his becoming the only Notre Dame back ever to gain more than 200 yards three times in a single season. He blasted off—and through—Pitt for 262 yards, Navy for 221 and Stanford for 218, leading the Irish to victory in each of those games. It was a triple play unlike anything a running back had been able to pull off in Notre Dame's storied history.

"I never felt I'd be lucky enough to do that," Jones said, after wrapping up his unprecedented hat trick in Notre Dame's dazzling 57-7 stampede over Stanford. "When I heard [in 2002] that I couldn't come back to Notre Dame, it really hurt. Looking back, it was the kick in the pants I needed to grow up and be a man."

Jones realized that finding a way to finish what he started, at the place where he started it, was the only road to redemption—not just for the NFL career prospects he almost frittered away, but for himself. With the help of his brother Thomas, an NFL running back, Jones started a triple assault on the comeback road: academically, athletically and personally. It took that blend of will and skill to seal this talented tailback's own special place in the Irish record book.

With typical reserve, Willingham waited for Jones to prove his worth at first, declining to list him as a team leader during preseason workouts. A few months later, when Jones's dedication was beyond dispute, the coach validated the impact he had on the rest of the team.

"It would have been easy for Julius to go somewhere else," Willingham pointed out. "He set a goal, committing himself to Notre Dame and his family. He's a leader, not just for performance on the field, but for the way his strength of spirit rubs off on the other players."

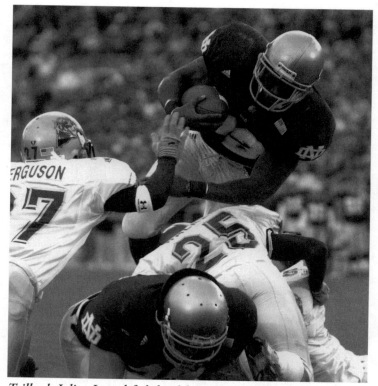

Tailback Julius Jones left behind lots of would-be tacklers and some remarkable rushing records in his final Notre Dame season.

Going the Distance

When Julius Jones returned a Nebraska kickoff 100 yards for a touchdown in 2000, Irish fans believed the brilliant tailback would kick off a new century of excellence at an old Notre Dame tradition—running the football. Nobody knew then what a long, hard journey Jones would face before scoring a crowd-pleasing touchdown, three years later, on his last carry in Notre Dame Stadium. It was a story of perseverance, courage and determination that made Irish fans realize that they had seen a running back blossom into true greatness

So when Jones arose to accept his award as the National Monogram Club's most valuable Irish player of 2003 at the team's annual banquet, he got an emotional standing ovation. It was a deserved tribute for a man who grew up in a hurry, turning his life and his career around, after leaving Notre Dame for a year.

Jones shared the spotlight that night with another Irish legend, quarterback Joe Montana. Rousing the crowd with words, like he did with actions on the field, Montana paid tribute to Jones's comeback before giving returning players, along with Irish fans and alumni, a challenge to bring Notre Dame football back to the pinnacle.

"It's up to us to find a way," Montana said.

Great Expectations

In the shadow of Julius Jones's brilliance, it was easy to overlook Ryan Grant, who went from a 1,000-yard rusher in 2002 to Jones's top backup by the time the book closed on 2003. As a senior, Grant figures to lug both the football and Irish hopes for a bruising ground game in 2004. It can happen if the offensive line proves it can muscle behemoths from Michigan, USC, Tennessee and points east and west out of the way to open holes for Grant and protect sophomore quarterback Brady Quinn.

Center Bob Morton, the live wire of the Irish offensive line, wasted no time reaching for the leadership whip left behind by the graduation loss of front-liners like Jeff Faine.

"We came together through tough times," Morton said. "I apologized to Julius Jones after we lost at Syracuse, because everybody wanted to send him out a winner, especially the offensive line. You just have to block harder for a guy like that."

Still, Morton's not the only man who will cast a decisive vote on Willingham's promise to bounce back in the presidential election year of 2004. The outcome of that campaign depends as well on Brady Quinn, the young Irish quarterback who showed he's capable of turning into a candidate in another race sometime over the next three seasons. With continued improvement, it's possible his name will show up on the Heisman Trophy ballot.

"What the young players went through gave us more than experience," Quinn said of the body of work that left Notre Dame with a 5-7 record. "We're battle-tested, ready to come back and start winning."

Willingham chuckled ruefully when a veteran Irish observer noted that if Jones had one more year of eligibility, there might be two Heisman hopefuls on his 2004 roster.

"Julius won't be here, and that's the reality," he said. "And if you're talking about Quinn, there's no way we would burden a sophomore quarterback with that sort of expectation."

Irish Fans T It Up

Notre Dame fans wore their hopes on their chests in 2002, greeting Tyrone Willingham's arrival as head coach with a sea of green. They quickly snapped up every available T-shirt proclaiming "Return to Glory." A shrewd motivator, Willingham wasted no time stirring up enthusiasm for the green wave sweeping across the campus, swirling around the Golden Dome and spilling over onto the streets of South Bend.

"Notre Dame students are making a statement of support for us," he said. "It's up to the players to prove they deserve that kind of enthusiasm. They're telling us, 'We want you to be successful.'"

Willingham's troops got the message, turning that optimism to hysteria by winning their first eight games under his command. Some stumbles at the end did not quench the thirst for still more thunder, so the T-shirt blitz of 2003 carried the message, "There's a Magic in the Name."

The Legend Lives

Most players and fans getting their first glimpse of Notre Dame Stadium can't deny there's some sort of special feeling in the air. It's neither awe nor intimidation. What is it, coach Ty Willingham?

"I felt that aura when I came here [in 1976] to play for Michigan State," he replied. "Notre Dame is a special place. Our players live in the dormitories with the rest of the students, preserving the tradition of Notre Dame football as an important part of campus life

"Of course, winning is an essential part of that tradition."

More Important Victories

Notre Dame's impact on players who get a chance to became students and campus contributors is not something fans read about on the nation's sports pages.

Chances are Darrell Campbell would have become a defensive stalwart anywhere he chose to play college football. Northwestern's Gary Barnett originally chose Campbell, but then left to coach at Colorado, so the suburban Chicago prospect ended up on the Irish roster. It took lots of persistence by Greg Mattison, the defensive line coach and recruiting coordinator, who figured this young man was worth the effort.

"I went back again to see Darrell wrestle in high school, even though he was learning toward Northwestern," Mattison said. "I believe Notre Dame needs kids with his kind of character."

Campbell was not an overnight success for the Irish, slowed by some injuries and position switches. When Ty Willingham arrived in as head coach in 2002, the youngster blossomed, providing two years of outstanding performance at defensive tackle. More to the point, Campbell's growth as an individual and a team leader outstripped his progress on the field.

"We'll keep looking for young men like Darrell Campbell," Willingham vowed.

Sports Showplace

When the Guglielmino Family Athletics Center opens on campus in 2005, it will be a haven for members of Notre Dame's 26 varsity teams in all sports. The $21.5 million building offers 95,840 square feet of space on two floors, providing state-of-the-art facilities for training, strength and conditioning, study and dining. It has separate areas for the football locker room, meeting rooms, recruiting lounge and coaches' offices.

"This center will have an enormous impact on all our student-athletes, particularly the Irish football team," said Kevin White, Notre Dame's athletic director.

All in the Family

A Notre Dame football tradition continued when Tregg Duerson joined the 2004 recruiting class. The running back from Chicago's Loyola Academy will be a defensive back for the Irish, following in the footsteps of his father, Dave. The elder Duerson was a hard-hitting Notre Dame safety in 1979-82, then joined the Chicago Bears (1983-89) to become a vital cog in the ferocious 46 defense that won the 1985 NFL championship and Super Bowl XX.

"My chest is puffed out with pride," said the successful Chicago businessman, who is on Notre Dame's board of trustees. Tregg Duerson can attest to that.

"Dad got real excited when Coach Willingham called to offer me a scholarship," Tregg said. "He started jumping around and pulling out old Notre Dame books and pictures."

CHAPTER 12

The Greatest Games

The games the Irish play seem to mean more to more people. In that sense, every game in the shadow of the Golden Dome and under the arms of Touchdown Jesus is a Big Game. Understandably, some are bigger than others. For instance ...

Notre Dame 10, Michigan State 10
Spartan Stadium, East Lansing, Michigan, November 19, 1966

How big was the 1966 battle of unbeatens between 9-0 Michigan State and 8-0 Notre Dame?

It loomed large enough that 26 years after the fact, it prompted Notre Dame alumnus Mike Celizic, a columnist for *The Record* of Bergen County, New Jersey, to write an entire book, *The Biggest Game of Them All*, about that single contest.

While games of the century are commonplace these days, that was one of the first to qualify legitimately as a late-season matchup between unbeatens. Neither team played in a bowl game that year—Michigan State had gone to the Rose Bowl after the '65 season and Big Ten rules prevented league teams from playing in Pasadena in successive years; Notre Dame at that time did not entertain bowl opportunities, though the 1966 season played a role in convincing the Notre Dame administration that playing in bowl games could be a positive factor in winning championships.

The coverage of the contest (headlines read "Notre Dame runs out clock" and "Old Notre Dame will tie over all") by *Sports Illustrated* frustrated Notre Dame students enough that a group of them (students claimed 200 participants; police suggested the number was 30) lit a bonfire in front of the Rockne Memorial Gymnasium and burned copies of the magazine.

Police categorized the demonstration as unlawful assembly and broke up the rally just as it started, apparently without any arrests made.

Said student spokesman Ed Kinle of Corry, Pennsylvania, "They were very unfair to Notre Dame. We were playing our second team. Five of our starters were out with injuries. I think Duffey Daugherty considers himself lucky he didn't lose."

State of Inflation

Tickets for the epic 1966 clash between Notre Dame and Michigan State went for $5 (face value). Tickets on the open market were going for $25, $50 and even—heaven forbid, in those days—$100 per seat.

Compare that with a $5 season ticket—hawked personally by Knute Rockne—in 1919 that provided admission to four football games, eight basketball games, four track meets and 10 baseball games.

In-Demand Television

Modern-day college football fans, used to oodles of televised games every weekend, would have had a hard time understanding the constraints of the 1960s when the NCAA controlled TV rights for college football. Teams were limited to three appearances in two seasons, and since Notre Dame's early-season home win over Purdue in 1966 had been nationally televised, that meant the best that could happen for the November clash between the unbeaten Irish and Michigan State Spartan clubs was a regional telecast.

ABC Sports announced it would, for the first time, show a Saturday doubleheader (USC vs. UCLA for the Rose Bowl invitation was the nightcap). ABC planned to show a different game than Notre Dame-Michigan State in the South (Tennessee-Kentucky) and Pacific Northwest (California-Stanford) regions, but it finally compromised by showing the contest on a tape-delay basis in those areas after receiving 50,000 pieces of complaint mail. The game drew a 22.5 rating, highest in history at that time for a college game.

Said Beano Cook, longtime ABC college football publicist:

"They put my name in a newspaper in Portland as the person to complain to and I received 350 letters, some telegrams and 19 long-distance phone calls—some collect—in three days, all pleading for a change."

"We get complaints every week, but this is the largest amount of frustration—not anger, but frustration—that we've had since the beginning of college telecasts."

Pregame Air Raid

Michigan State students wore "Kill, Bubba, Kill" buttons (they were produced by Smith's roommate). State students referred to their top weapon (defensive end Bubba Smith) as Intercontinental Ballistic Bubba. At 6'7" and 283 pounds, he was a relative giant in his time (he wore a 52 extra long suit).

Other Spartan fans rented a plane that dropped leaflets on the Notre Dame campus to warn students (the Peace-Loving Villagers of Notre Dame):

"Our friends, why do you struggle against us? Why do you persist in the mistaken belief that you can win freely and openly against us?

"Your leaders have lied to you. They have led you to believe you are more powerful than we. They have led you to believe you can win. They have given you false hopes. They have deceived their own people.

"We have nothing but affection for Notre Dame."

It was signed, "A free message from the Michigan State University of America."

Notre Dame 35, Houston 34
Cotton Bowl, Dallas, Texas, January 1, 1979

Notre Dame's 1979 Cotton Bowl victory may not have carried the national significance of the 38-10 Irish victory a year earlier, which clinched the national championship for Dan Devine's team. But more than a quarter-century later, New Year's Day, 1979, stands out as the greatest comeback in Notre Dame history. In fact, it ranks near the top for late-game heroics in college football annals.

Ninth-ranked Notre Dame's trip to Dallas followed a tough road loss to USC that dropped the defending national champions to 8-3 on the season. The Cotton Bowl opponent, Houston, was the Southwest Conference champion.

The weather in Dallas was uncharacteristically cold. The Irish arrived at the Cotton Bowl facility to find machines clearing ice and snow off the field. The slush clearly affected the teams' play for the first three quarters—the game's first six scores were the result of turnovers. And Irish quarterback Joe Montana, who had already been intercepted four times, was forced to sit out most of the third quarter when his body temperature dropped to 96 degrees.

Dr. Les Bodnar, Notre Dame's team physician, always kept chicken soup in an emergency pack on the sideline. Bodnar warmed up the soup and fed it at halftime to Montana, who was wrapped in blankets. By the time Montana returned, the Irish were down 34-12, a score that still stood with 7:30 remaining.

The comeback began when Tony Belden blocked a punt and Steve Cichy returned it for a touchdown. Montana followed by hitting Vagas Ferguson for the two-point conversion. After a defensive stop, Montana drove the Irish downfield, scored himself on a two-yard run and hit Kris Haines in the end zone for another two-point conversion. With 4:15 remaining, the Irish closed the gap to 34-28.

A defensive stand gave Notre Dame the ball at the Houston 49 with 2:25 to play. After Notre Dame moved to the 36, Montana scrambled for what would have been a 16-yard gain, except the quarterback was stripped of the ball, giving possession back to the Cougars with 2:05 remaining.

"Even some of my best friends turned off their television at that point," Devine later wrote in his autobiography.

The Irish stopped the Cougars on the first three downs, then went offsides trying to block the punt on fourth and six. But Joe Gramke and Mike Calhoun stopped Houston's Emmett King, giving the Irish the ball with 28 seconds remaining.

Montana scrambled for 11 yards, then hit Haines with a 10-yard pass. Haines stepped out of bounds at the eight with six seconds left on the clock. Montana then grounded the ball after the first play didn't develop, leaving two seconds for a final pass. With no time left Montana hit Haines in the end zone to tie the game at 34. Walk-on kicker Joe Unis drilled the extra point for the win, but there was a flag. Offsides. But Unis hit his second try, giving the Irish an improbable comeback victory.

The comeback was later featured in a movie narrated by Harry Caray called *Seven and One-half Minutes to Destiny*.

"If I were the owner or CEO of a pro football team or had an expansion club," Devine said after the game, "and the ruling was that I could have for my first pick all of the current players in the NFL and all of the players coming out of college, I would use that number-one pick for Joe Montana."

Faust Fodder

Notre Dame 23, Michigan 17
Notre Dame Stadium, September 18, 1982

We opened my second season at Notre Dame with a first for the Irish, a night game at Notre Dame Stadium. Our opponent, Michigan, topped us 25-7 the previous year in front of more than 105,000 fans in the Big House. The game was on national television and we had some extra motivation in Michigan coach Bo Schembechler, who said he would never lose to a high school coach.

The game was electrifying. Not even a terrible quirk of fate could keep us from victory. But it did make me say to myself: Don't tell me we're going to lose again. It happened with 7:38 to play in the fourth quarter. Michigan quarterback Steve Smith, throwing from our 39, found freshman Gilvanni Johnson at the 25. As Johnson caught the ball, Stacey Toran and Dave Duerson sandwiched him with such hard hits that

Johnson should have felt like a piece of pressed meat. The ball popped out of Johnson's hands and came to rest on Toran's shoulder. Instead of falling harmlessly to the ground, however, it was snatched by Michigan's Rick Rogers, who ran in for a touchdown. Believe it or not, I was speechless.

We held on for a 23-17 victory, when Duerson picked off a pass with about two minutes to play. As I had the year before, when I was suffering my first loss as a college head coach, I ran across the field to shake Bo Schembechler's hand. Guess what? No Bo.

He had stormed to the Michigan locker room. I guess losing to a high school coach was more than he could take. I could understand why he was upset. I like Bo. He's a dynamic person and a great competitor. But I can say I never ran off without shaking the other coach's hand. That isn't the way they taught us to do it in high school.

Notre Dame 31, Pittsburgh 16
Pitt Stadium, Pittsburgh, Pennsylvania,
November 6, 1982

We'd started out 4-0 in my second year as coach and moved into the top 10 before losing 16-13 to unranked Arizona at home on October 16. We followed that with a 13-13 tie against unranked Oregon. A win over Navy the next week wasn't enough to get us back into the rankings.

We opened November with the No. 1 team in the country, Dan Marino's Pittsburgh Panthers. Marino had future NFL stars Bill Fralic and Jimbo Covert blocking for him, and excellent receivers such as Dwight Collins and Julius Dawkins for targets. We concluded we weren't going to stop Marino, so we decided to take away the deep pass. If Marino was going to air it out successfully, he was going to throw short.

On offense, we noted two keys. Pitt played a lot of man-to-man coverage and had trouble covering backs running pass routes out of the backfield. In addition, their free safety, Thomas Flynn, reacted quickly—maybe too quickly—to stop the run.

After we warmed up the next day and headed for our locker room in Pitt Stadium, there waiting for us by the door was Keith Penrod in his wheelchair. Keith was a man of about 30 who lived in South Bend. His whole life was Notre Dame football. He was born with a handicap that made it difficult for him to speak. He talked out of the side of his mouth, and when he got excited and talked fast he could be difficult to understand. The players understood Keith, though. They loved him.

Keith was always welcome with our team, but he had told no one he was coming to Pittsburgh. When the players saw him sitting there in his wheelchair with this big smile on his face, they went bonkers.

"Keith," I said. "How did you get here?"

"I took a Greyhound bus," he said.

"Well," I said. "you're not taking any bus home. You're flying with us. Now you come into the locker room."

If seeing Keith Penrod and knowing the effort he had made to get to Pittsburgh to be with us weren't enough, I added some pregame fuel to the players' fire.

"Today," I told the team in the locker room before the game, "we're playing the No. 1 team in the country in its stadium. It's November 6, 1982, and you're going to go down in the annals of Notre Dame as the eighth team with a great upset of a No. 1 team. You are about to carry on a Notre Dame tradition."

Those weren't just words.

Our game plan worked perfectly, if a little late. Keeping Marino's receivers in front of us, we did not allow a touchdown pass despite giving up 314 yards. In the fourth quarter, we used the flea-flicker to take advantage of their free safety. The irony is, Pitt's starting free safety, Flynn, had been injured, but the play worked anyway because his replacement played the same aggressive, come-up-fast-to-stop-the-run game.

The first time we had the ball in the last quarter, Blair Kiel handed off to tailback Phil Carter and the safety took the bait. As he rushed to the line of scrimmage, Joe Howard streaked past him and Carter turned and pitched the ball to Kiel. Blair threw 54 yards to Howard, who scored untouched.

Marino wasn't finished, but cornerback Chris Brown knocked down one key pass and then our other cornerback, John Mosley, recovered a fumble. Meanwhile, freshman Allen Pinkett was having his second consecutive 100-yard game—this one 112 yards on 10 carries—including touchdown runs of 76 and seven yards in the fourth quarter.

The locker room was a scene I'll never forget. I gave one of the game balls to Keith Penrod, and the players went crazy. And you should have seen Keith. Of all the things I've done, I probably got more from the look on his face when he received that football than anything else. He still has the keepsake from one of Notre Dame's greatest victories.

When we arrived back in South Bend, there were 10,000 to 15,000 people waiting for us on Notre Dame Avenue as we rolled up in three buses. It took us longer to travel the one mile to the circle on campus than it had to drive from the airport to the campus.

I was standing in the front seat of the bus and people were pounding on the outside. When we stopped, they climbed on top of the bus. They were cheering.

The street was jammed. They were singing the Notre Dame Victory March. I spoke at that impromptu pep rally that broke out when we got out of our buses and were swallowed up by the cheering crowd.

"It was by far," Father Joyce said years later, "Gerry's greatest victory. That was the high point—but nobody knew it at the time."

Notre Dame 19, Boston College 18
Liberty Bowl, Memphis, Tennessee,
December 29, 1983

We received some criticism for accepting an invitation from Bud Dudley—a Notre Dame alumnus and executive director of the Liberty Bowl at the time—to take on Boston College in the 1983 game in Memphis. At that time, if Notre Dame was good enough, it attracted big bowls. If the team wasn't good enough to go to a major bowl game, Notre Dame had a habit of just saying no.

But because of Bud Dudley—and because I badly wanted to go to a bowl—we accepted the invitation before our November 19 season finale against Air Force. We lost that game when Mike Johnston's field goal was blocked with four seconds left, and the criticism only got worse.

We were going to a bowl game at 6-5. To top it off, our opponent in what some dubbed the "Catholic Bowl" was a 9-2 Boston College team led by Heisman Trophy winner Doug Flutie at quarterback.

Two things stand out when I remember the 1983 Liberty Bowl—senior Blair Kiel's performance and the weather. How cold was it?

That was the only time at Notre Dame that I wore a hat on the sideline. At Moeller, before the state championship game in 1975, Father Tedesco's dad gave me a hat. I wore it that cold day, and we won 14-13. In the next five years, we played for the state championship four times. I only wore a hat on the sidelines for those five state championship games, and we never lost. I sure would have liked to have taken a shot at wearing a hat while coaching on the Notre Dame sidelines and seeing if our record would have been better. Maybe that's one of the mistakes I made while I was coaching.

While the weather made life miserable for the 47,071 in the stands, it did little to stop our running game. Allen Pinkett totaled 111 yards, while Chris Smith added 104 yards on 18 carries. Each scored one touchdown.

Blair, a former starter relegated to a backup role after the first three games of the season, earned the start after a solid performance off the bench against Air Force and came on strong in his final game at Notre Dame. He completed 11 of 19 passes for 151 yards and one touchdown. Flutie threw for 287 yards, but it wasn't quite enough.

We led 19-12 at halftime. A Flutie touchdown pass midway through the third quarter closed the gap to one, but the Eagles failed on a two-point conversion and we held them the rest of the way.

Afterward, for only the second time in my career, some of the players lifted me on their shoulders and carried me to the center of the field to shake hands with Boston College coach Jack Bicknell. It was a great feeling.

✝

Notre Dame 31, Florida State 24
Notre Dame Stadium, November 13, 1993

Maybe the 1988 triumph over Miami was more important or more memorable, or both, for the Irish and their legion of lifetime fans. But there was just as much at stake in this collision with Florida State. A pregame headline said it all: "Clash of the Titans." It certainly was all that and more. The Irish proved they were a better team on offense and defense, but it still came down to last-play heroics, just like the 31-30 Miami thriller. After Shawn Wooden batted down Florida State quarterback Charlie Ward's last-gasp bid for the tying touchdown, a tidal wave of jubilation swept over the stadium walls, throughout Indiana and across the country, wherever Irish fans huddled around their TV sets to sweat through those fingernail-gnawing final minutes. The final gun triggered bedlam on the field, plus what Lou Holtz had warned against a few days earlier—overconfidence. Notre Dame leapfrogged over the Seminoles into the No. 1 poll spot, pointing toward its second national championship in five years.

"Are they going to award the title to the winner of this game?" Holtz wanted to know. "If not, we haven't won anything yet."

Who's No. 2?

As fate would have it, he was right. At this moment of supreme ecstasy, however, there was no way to imagine the agony that awaited the Irish just one week later. Meanwhile, Florida State's players and fans were in the depths of despair.

"Feels like somebody tore my heart out and shot my dog," said Florida State center Clay Shiver.

He got no sympathy from crowds whooping it up on the campus and in South Bend's booming bars and restaurants. But

Seminoles fans felt Shiver's pain, seeking solace from each other in person and on the phone. One Florida State alum called his father in Florida during the game to lament that a cold wind, drizzly weather and slippery turf were slowing down their team, used to rolling up yardage and points under ideal conditions in the Sunshine State.

"That's not the worst part," his dad said. "They're going against Touchdown Jesus. I've been hearing about that Notre Dame mystique for years, and now I'm starting to believe it."

The Day the Music Died

Not just Irish fans, but the college football world in general cut loose with a unanimous, "Well, there he goes again," when Lou Holtz cautioned that Boston College would not be a pushover. After all, the Irish had routed the Eagles, 54-7, in their last meeting. Coming off a near-perfect effort that knocked Florida State from its No. 1 perch, all they had to do was ground the Eagles to wrap up an unbeaten season and take a shot at the 1993 crown.

"We've got to play better, because I would be tempted to put Boston College No. 1 this week," Holtz said.

Boston College 41, Notre Dame 39
Notre Dame Stadium, November 20, 1993

More than a decade later, little can be said that hasn't been spoken or written about one of the most unbelievable football games ever played in a place where miracle finishes seem almost routine. Notre Dame, playing from behind most of the day, came roaring back in the closing minutes with a display of awesome power, precision and pluck. Trailing 38-17 in the fourth quarter, quarterback Kevin McDougal somehow pulled off a brilliant series of scoring drives. McDougal capped it with a fourth-down bullet pass to Lake Dawson, who was racing across the end zone's back line. Suddenly, the Irish led 39-38, and the dream was alive and well. Then, with just over a minute to go, Eagles quarterback Glenn Foley put together one more miracle drive, setting up possibly the saddest moment in a half-century plus of ups and downs in Notre Dame Stadium. When David Gordon's left-footed, wounded-duck, 41-yard field goal trickled over the crossbar for the crushing points, it was the all-time downer for the Irish. In that instant, an entire season of maximum effort vanished.

Pete Won't Retreat

Pete Bercich sat at his locker in Notre Dame's disconsolate dressing room, crying for 15 minutes. Then he went out to meet the media. The classy senior stayed there until the last interrogator left, answering the same question over and over: "What happened on that interception?" It didn't happen, because Bercich had the game-saving theft in his hands, but couldn't hold on. So Boston College, given still more life, kept rolling toward the fatal field goal.

When David Gordon's knuckleball went through, it could have been the start of something bad for Bercich. Instead, he used that tough experience to make life easier on himself. The burly linebacker learned to hold his temper—and his tongue—when occasional sore losers or rub-it-in types insisted on trying to reopen the old scar.

"So I'm still the goat, even though I busted my hump for four years at Notre Dame," Bercich said, with a resigned shrug. "In a situation like that, you do or you don't. I didn't, we lost and life goes on. The success we had all through that season is what I'd prefer to dwell on, not the one failure."

Pete Bercich celebrates an interception against Northwestern. Despite a dropped potential interception in the 1993 Boston College heartbreak, Bercich had a standout Irish career.

Bercich went on to a seven-year NFL career with the Minnesota Vikings. Whenever the Irish of 1993 get together, the former linebacker still slips easily into his dual roles as an on-the-field-leader and the life of the party when the storytelling begins.

Michigan 26, Notre Dame 24
Notre Dame Stadium, September 10, 1994

Remy Hamilton's field goal was just a yard shorter than the one David Gordon booted in Notre Dame's previous home game. Gordon's 41-yarder kicked the Irish a little harder in the heart, because it gave Boston College the 41-39 victory that ruined Notre Dame's chances for the 12th national championship it hungered for. That didn't make this last-second shocker any easier to take.

Some theorized that another field goal—the one that gave Air Force a 20-17 overtime upset in 1996—was the last straw for coach Lou Holtz. Regardless, the pair by Gordon and Hamilton, nullifying 60 minutes of gut-wrenching effort by the Irish, took more of an emotional toll on Holtz than it did on his players. The Irish seemed ready to move past the Boston College debacle by routing Northwestern, 42-15, behind a splendid passing performance from Ron Powlus. It was an impressive 1994 debut for Powlus and his team before a sellout Soldier Field crowd of 66,946.

All that changed a week later, in the twinkling of Hamilton's toe. It was doubly excruciating, because the Irish had fought back to a 24-23 lead on a seven-yard touchdown pass from Powlus to Derrick Mayes.

The Notre Dame score happened on first down, with 51 seconds to go. It gave the Wolverines time enough to move 59 yards in 50 seconds, setting up for the clincher on the final tick. The key play leading up to the field goal was an escape act by Michigan quarterback Todd Collins. With blitzing Irish linebacker Bert Berry draped all over him, Collins somehow flipped a desperation pass to Seth Smith, keeping the final drive alive.

Hamilton's 42-yard game winner sailed through with plenty to spare, unlike the Gordon wobbler that refused to fall short. Either way, both boots drew the same reaction from a grim-faced Holtz.

"Devastating," he said.

"We always believe in miracles here," said linebacker Jeremy Nau, reflecting the postgame gloom shrouding the Irish. "But they're supposed to happen for Notre Dame."

Notre Dame 27, Texas 24
Darrell K. Royal-Texas Stadium,
September 21, 1996

Everything's bigger in Texas, pardner. When the Irish got their kicks deep in the heart of Texas, thanks to a last-second field goal, it was gigantic letdown for the Longhorns. This clash between unbeatens, billed as the "Game of the Century" in Austin, rose above that hyperbole to earn legitimate status as a classic. Texas, ranked No. 6 early in '96, wanted revenge for the previous season's 55-27 humiliation in Notre Dame Stadium, and Longhorns coach John Mackovic had the horses to bid for a national title this time.

Jim Sanson's 39-yard boot burst that bubble, capping a closing Irish comeback that surpassed blockbuster TV oil opera *Dallas* for sheer drama. It was a high-intensity thriller, riveting the sweltering, stadium-record throng of 83,312, including then-Texas governor George W. Bush and his wife, Laura.

"Notre Dame's no better than New Mexico State," grumbled Longhorns tackle Clarence Martin, echoing the sweaty sour grapes oozing from their departing fans.

Heaven Helps Lou

"It's hard to see the winning kick go through when you're staring straight up at the sky," said Lou Holtz, looking for all the help he could get to bring the Irish back in Texas Stadium, where he'd been beaten in all three previous visits as Arkansas coach. "God didn't put me on earth to lose four straight times in this place."

One glance at Holtz during the postgame wrapup gave the media inquisitors some evidence of the strain on the coach's gaunt face. The Irish were 3-0 at that moment, so nobody could have guessed Holtz would resign just before the 1996 season ended.

"Our dream is alive," exulted linebacker Lyron Cobbins, who made the game-turning interception in the closing minutes. "We're in the national championship hunt."

Notre Dame 21, Navy 17
Notre Dame Stadium, November 1, 1997

For wild, weird finishes, this one has to rank near the top 10, even though strange things happen routinely in the House that Rockne built. On Halloween weekend, a scary bounce almost handed Navy a spooky last-second victory. Trailing 21-17, Middies quarterback Chris McCoy launched a desperation pass into the gathering murk and mist of a soggy late afternoon.

An unseen hand made the wet pigskin bounce off the helmet of Irish safety Deke Cooper, right to Middies receiver Pat McGrew. He wasn't too startled to hotfoot down the left sideline, only to get bumped out of bounds by speedy pursuer Allen Rossum's game-saving tackle, just short of the goal line.

"I thought Halloween was over," said Notre Dame coach Bob Davie, hair still standing on end.

Notre Dame 36, Michigan 20
Notre Dame Stadium, September 5, 1998

None of the previous battles between these perennial powers ended up this one-sided. Michigan, still brooding about the vote-splitting that cost the Wolverines an undisputed 1997 national championship, came in determined to win it all. Brushing aside the Irish seemed like far from the hardest part of that agenda. The Wolverines led, 13-6, at halftime, but they got burned by a 17-0 firestorm in the third quarter. Irish tailback Autry Denson demolished their defense, rushing for a career-high 162 yards and a pair of touchdowns.

"It was time to put our hearts out there and play some execution football," Denson said.

The Irish offense did just that, and Michigan paid the price.

Notre Dame 31, Boston College 26
Alumni Stadium, Chestnut Hill, Massachusetts,
November 7, 1998

It took five years for Notre Dame to even the score—partially, at least—with Boston College. Nothing could completely ease the pain of the Eagles' catastrophic 41-39 upset victory in 1993, but this magnificent 1998 goal line stand sure helped. Stuffing any opponent in that situation, to prevent a win from getting snatched away in the closing seconds, would be memorable. But this was Boston College, the foe that derailed Notre Dame's national championship hopes in 1993. So getting even by preventing this bitter rival from gaining those last few inches for the final touchdown made for one of the brightest moments in Bob Davie's five-year coaching regime.

The Irish had boosted their lead to five points before Boston College launched what looked like a rerun of its relentless 1993 closing drive. But with Notre Dame leading by five, this was different—a touchdown or nothing. The Eagles soared from their 23-yard line to first and goal at Notre Dame's four, with 1:07. That was enough time to run four plays, the last two from inside the one.

"All we said to each other was 'Stop them here or go home crying, like we did in 1993,'" said nose tackle Antwon Jones. "Notre Dame and Boston College never did like each other, but ever since that game, the intensity is unbelievable."

Especially for Jones and the other seniors, who had played alongside some of the 1993 starters. Those friendships transferred the pain of the Boston College ambush, so Autry Denson, Mike Rosenthal, Lamont Bryant and the other upperclassmen made sure the younger players knew why this game was an out-and-out grudge match. With a hostile throng bellowing in their ears, the Irish took an all-or-nothing gamble on third down. Boston College stopped the clock to set up the fourth thrust. Fortunately for the weary bodies of the Irish and the battered spirit of their fans, the decision was to swing the sledgehammer one more time.

"I was afraid their quarterback [Scott Mutryn] would fake the handoff, bootleg wide and walk into the end zone." said Davie, a longtime defensive coordinator. "But we told the DBs to ignore the pass and blitz all-out at the snap."

Safety Deke Cooper followed instructions. He roared through the line, slamming into halfback Mike Cloud's belly as soon as Mutryn put the football there for the last charge. Cooper's jarring tackle stopped Cloud behind the line and launched his Notre Dame teammates onto cloud nine.

Notre Dame 34, Oklahoma 30
Notre Dame Stadium, October 2, 1999

Bob Stoops wasted no time proving he's a fast learner. In only his second year as head coach at Oklahoma, he steered the Sooners to the 2000 national championship. In 1999, the coach's first season, the former Iowa defensive back installed a high-powered scoring machine that saw quarterback Josh Heupel need just four games to break Oklahoma's single-season record of 14 touchdown passes. So when unbeaten Oklahoma stormed into Notre Dame Stadium in 1999 to renew a storied intersectional rivalry, Irish fans feared the worst.

Never known for suffering in silence, they fretted out loud when Heupel passed the visitors into a 30-14 third-quarter lead. But the best quarterback on the field that day was just getting warmed up. Jarious Jackson put on a show in the final 20 minutes that ranks with the best ever seen in Notre Dame Stadium.

He engineered three straight textbook touchdown thrusts and the Irish soared to a 34-30 triumph on the wings of that 20-0 blitzkrieg.

"If I needed IVs or anything else, nothing was going to stop me," an exhausted Jackson said. "I had to be a warrior, all-out on every play."

He was, and Stoops agreed Jackson made the difference.

"He made us look foolish, running around us or over us," the Sooners' coach said. "Notre Dame's will to win was stronger than ours, but Jackson was the main factor."

Notre Dame 34, Florida State 24
Doak Campbell Stadium, October 26, 2002

The Notre Dame faithful speedily nominated Tyrone Willingham for the legendary coaches' wing of the Notre Dame football Hall of Fame after the new sheriff in town had master-minded a mere seven games. The fact that the Irish won all seven might have had something to do with it. Despite all that euphoria on the home front, the rest of the country seemed to rank the rejuvenated Irish somewhere between a rumor and a mirage.

So Willingham's ability to walk on water was supposed to end abruptly when he took his team to Tallahassee to resume an intersectional feud with Florida State. The Irish didn't expect a welcome wagon to roll out for them, and most of the 84,106 spectators figured they would get rolled over. After all, the Seminoles had not lost a nonconference home game to an opponent from outside Florida since 1984. And in two meetings since their memorable 1993 Notre Dame Stadium showdown, Florida State pulled out a pair of tough victories, in 1994 and 1995.

"Nobody believes in us except us," said Irish linebacker Courtney Watson. "We have to go down there and change some perceptions."

All it took was a lightning stretch of the third quarter for the Irish to profit from Watson's prophecy.

The Irish scored 17 points in only two minutes and 21 seconds, and just like that, it was a semi-blowout. Bowden, the canny coach of the Seminoles, summed up the reaction of fans unused to seeing someone do to them what they'd been doing to opponents for years. "Notre Dame had us bumfuzzled all day," Bowden confessed.

CHAPTER 13

The Irish Spirit

United We Stand

Notre Dame absorbed the shock of September 11, 2001, with the same resiliency that brought the rest of the country together to share grief, outrage and determination.

Along with most postponed college games, the Irish trip to Purdue, originally scheduled for September 15, was rescheduled for December 1, a 24-18 victory in Bob Davie's final game as head coach.

Life, including games, went on after another week of national soul-searching and resolve. When Michigan State came to Notre Dame Stadium on September 22, an impressive display of patriotic fervor paid tribute to the victims and saluted the heroes who died trying to save them. Playing despite lumps in their throats, both teams agreed that watching fans wave 80,000 cardboard replica American flags, provided by the *South Bend Tribune*, was an emotional experience. During the game, spectators contributed money and prayers for the families of New York police and firefighters. The right note of national unity was sounded at halftime, when the Michigan State and Notre Dame bands mingled on the field to play "Amazing Grace."

Rockne's House Still Home, Sweet Home

It took a threat to quit by Knute Rockne for Notre Dame to consider building a new stadium. The legendary Irish coach had a point. His Four Horsemen had to score most of their points on the road, because antiquated Cartier Field's wooden stands seated only 30,000.

"Our football team puts on a first-rate production in a third-rate setting," Rockne complained.

So with design tips from the coach, Notre Dame Stadium was built for a bargain-basement price of less than $800,000 and opened for business in 1930, as the Great Depression tightened its grip on America.

Rockne got to coach only five games there before his death in a 1931 place crash. He and 4-0 Ed McKeever, the 1944 fill-in while Frank Leahy was in the Navy, are the only Irish coaches unbeaten at home. The red brick and limestone showplace provided plenty of thrills and chills over the next 66 years after Rockne's national champs edged SMU, 20-14, in the first Notre Dame Stadium game on October 4, 1930. Rock and the 11 Irish coaches who succeeded him compiled a combined 255-75-5 record there through 1996, Lou Holtz's final season.

By then, construction was well under way for an overdue expansion. The familiar 59,075 attendance figure would get a big boost with the addition of 26 rows atop the old stadium, part of an extensive $53 million renovation. With a new coach, Bob Davie, at the controls, new-look Notre Dame Stadium made its debut on September 6, 1997, when the Irish squeaked past Georgia Tech, 17-13. The new seating capacity, 80,795, still fell short of the demand for tickets.

Young Knute Rockne, shown here in his student days, prepares to bring worldwide fame to Notre Dame.

SC's Always a Must-See

Midwest and Big Ten rivalries are important to Notre Dame. Their in-state battles with Purdue have had national championship implications over the years, as have long-running series with Michigan and Michigan State. Other least favorite opponents, notably Florida State and Miami, periodically pop up on the most-wanted list of devout Irish fans.

Boston College is always there, thanks to the friendly greetings Eagles rooters extend whenever Notre Dame ventures into New England. Ditto, to a slightly lesser extent, for Pittsburgh.

But when it comes down to take-no-prisoners intersectional warfare with all the traditional trimmings, Southern California is the place and the Trojans are the team. Since this semi-annual Tinseltown Tour was first booked in 1926, it's become a game that makes coast-to-coast headlines.

"That game meant more than others, because alumni from both schools were choosing up sides all over the country," said Pat Terrell, starting safety on the 1988 Irish national champions. "Coach [Lou] Holtz used his whole bag of psychological tricks to get us pumped up for USC. Not that he needed to, with so much riding on those games. He had the USC fight song blaring through loudspeakers at practice, so loud we could hardly hear each other in the huddle."

Big Ten and Out

Sports, like life, goes in cycles. In the 1920s, Notre Dame wanted to join the Big Ten, but the conference deemed the Irish unworthy. The transformation from arrogance to acceptance took more than a half-century. Notre Dame had grown into the most recognizable name in college athletics, with a lucrative NBC television contract, a solid base of nationwide fans and mass marketing appeal, thanks to a football tradition equal to that of any team in the Big Ten.

So when the conference floated trial balloons in the late 1990s, the reply was a predictable, "Thanks, but no thanks." Not that Notre Dame's becoming the 12th member of the 11-team Big Ten lacked a powerful upside. Both academically and athletically, blending into this prestigious group of universities would have enhanced the private school's options in many research and information-sharing areas. The downside was that Notre Dame's essentially Catholic character would have been under pressure, along with its unique image. The prospect of playing a full Big Ten football schedule also mandated painful cutbacks for the intersectional games that enabled Irish fans and alumni to see games in all parts of the country.

"Notre Dame has a distinct identity," said Rev. Edward A. Malloy, the university president, delivering the rejection a landslide majority of Irish students, alumni and fans made it clear they wanted.

"Differences between [us] and the Big Ten are essential, not incidental. Does this core identity seem a match for even a splendid association of great universities that are uniformly secular, predominantly state institutions? Our answer...is no."

Few dissenters to the go-it-alone choice could be found on the serene South Bend campus, or elsewhere.

"Notre Dame's commitment to students and spiritual atmosphere are very important," said Leticia Benitiz, a freshman from El Paso, Texas. "Football is a unifying force for us."

Shirley's Surely Irish

Notre Dame fans come in all shapes, sizes and age ranges. Not many of them display their Irish loyalty more clearly—and entertainingly—than Shirley Zultanski. This lifelong fan not only sings Notre Dame's praises, but writes the words she sings.

Shirley Zultanski not only sings Notre Dame's praises, but writes the words she sings.

It comes naturally to Shirley, because her parents were in vaudeville around Chicago before the family moved to South Bend in the 1930s, when she was just four years old. She's a longtime professional chanteuse, appearing with bands in clubs, at weddings and other events around Michiana, though always tuned to Irish games on fall Saturdays.

"I listened to Bob Lux on the radio," Shirley said of the WSBT-AM pregame show hosted for 30 years by that veteran of the airwaves. "Bob needed some music to liven things up, so I taped one of my Notre Dame songs and started appearing on his program."

Sure enough, Shirley's bubbly personality and catchy lyrics were a hit with Irish fans, tuning in while driving to Notre Dame Stadium. A sample, written and sung by her:

"We are Notre Dame fans, loyal to the Blue and Gold
You hear our voices ring, so confident and bold
We're cheering for the Irish as they march to world acclaim

The happiest people in the world are fans of Notre Dame."

Not surprisingly, Shirley and her husband, Walter, raised a musical family. Daughter Carol, a secretary in Notre Dame's sports information department, is a band singer, and daughter Bonnie, a Colorado resident, also sings.

Bright Idea

Light banks at the four corners of Notre Dame's revamped stadium and atop the enlarged press box are not for night games. They come in handy to ward off the swirling fog and mist of late November afternoons, when darkness creeps in to shroud the Touchdown Jesus mural.

"Our agreement with NBC assures that home football games won't be moved to prime time," said the Rev. Bill Beauchamp, then the university's executive vice president.

Green Light for White

Kevin White came to Notre Dame in 2000 with a reputation as a program doctor for colleges in all parts of the country. He is aware that football is the main priority for many Irish alumni and rooters from coast to coast and around the world. While keeping his eye on that prize, the athletic director sought national rankings for all Notre Dame sports and got it quickly from coach Muffet McGraw, when her women's basketball team won the 2001 NCAA Tournament. Still, he's a realist.

"Given Notre Dame's storied football history and tradition, you can't expect our other sports to be approached with egalitarianism," White conceded. "Football must be successful here."

Congratulations to a winner on the football field and most importantly in the game of life.

— *Peter and Celeste Spitalieri*

PASCO

140 Terex Road, Hudson, OH 44236 • (330) 655–7202
http://www.pasco-group.com/pasco/pascohome.html

/WWP